Sailing the Worldly Winds

A Buddhist Way through the Ups and Downs of Life

Vajragupta

T0162042

(W)indhorse Publications

Published by
Windhorse Publications
169 Mill Road
Cambridge
CB1 3AN
United Kingdom

info@windhorsepublications.com
www.windhorsepublications.com

First Edition 2011

Typeset and designed by Ben Cracknell Studios
Cover design by Deborah Harward
Cover image © Don Bayley
Printed by Bell & Bain Ltd, Glasgow

British Library Cataloguing in Publication Data:
A catalogue record for this book is available from the British Library

ISBN: 9781 907314 10 0

To my father

About the author

Vajragupta was born as Richard Staunton in 1968 and grew up in London. He studied social science at university and first came into contact with Buddhism at the Birmingham Buddhist Centre (a centre of the Triratna Buddhist Community) in the early 1990s. He was ordained in 1994 and given the name Vajragupta which means 'secret, or hidden, diamond-like truth'. He was director of the Birmingham Buddhist Centre from 1997 to 2005, and is now director of the Triratna Development Team – working for a collective of 50 Triratna centres and projects across Europe. He currently lives in Worcester, England, where he teaches Buddhism and meditation, enjoys walking and wildlife, reading, poetry, and travelling over to nearby Stratford to watch productions of Shakespeare plays. His previous books, *Buddhism: Tools for Living Your Life* and *The Triratna Story*, were also published by Windhorse Publications.

Contents

Acknowledgements

A number of people read the first draft of this book at quite short notice and gave very perceptive and helpful comments. I'd like to thank them: Liz Bayley, Larry Butler, Elaine Jackson, Kalyacitta, Norman Long, Mahasiddhi, Mokshini and Sarah Ryan. I've appreciated the editorial skill and judgement of Priyananda and Vidyadevi. The folk at Windhorse Publications were very patient when I didn't make the deadlines; my thanks to them for producing the book within a very tight schedule.

Introduction

At last I'd arrived. Now I could settle in, and get on with writing my book on the worldly winds. I'd managed to carve two weeks free in my busy diary, and a friend had allowed me to stay in his family's caravan in the countryside. I'd been looking forward to this writing project and it was such a relief to finally get down to it, and a pleasure to do so in a quiet place, in beautiful landscape.

Two days later my mum phoned, distressed, and said that my 89-year-old father had fallen over at home. He'd been taken into hospital for a few days. My dad had been poorly for some time, but suddenly he seemed much weaker.

I decided, with a heavy heart, to leave the caravan, to pack up my books and computer, and to go and spend a few days with my mum and dad. I travelled down to where they live and managed to speak to their doctor. My dad had stomach cancer, it had spread to other parts of his body, and there was nothing they could do. I asked how long he might have to live. The doctor said it was hard to say and was reluctant to give an answer. 'Will it be weeks or months?' I asked. It was a matter of weeks.

I spent as much of those next few weeks as I could with my parents. Since their flat is small, I booked into a local bed and breakfast. I spent the mornings in my little room with its clicking radiator and a sink with a plug-hole that gurgled every half hour.

I sat with my laptop computer perched on my knees and wrote this book. Around lunchtime I went round to my mum, ran some errands for her, and then we walked down the road to the hospital to see my dad.

At first the hospital was a strange, unknown place, but that little journey became very familiar. There was a tree where a robin often sang, even though it was mid-winter. There were the sliding doors of the hospital, and the beige walls of the long corridor. We'd walk past the TV room, the X-ray department, and the room from which an elderly woman always shouted 'Help, help, help, I need help', no matter how many times the staff went in to see her.

As William Blake wrote, joy and woe are woven fine. They were strange, sad, painful weeks. My dad became weaker and thinner, till he was too frail to stand, and his legs, arms and hands were like the legs and claws of a little bird. There was nothing we could do; we just watched him fading away.

They were also strangely inspiring and beautiful weeks. My dad seemed to accept what was happening with a quiet humility. He was uncomplaining and unfussy. He kept a sense of humour. I was with him once in hospital when a nurse came in with a needle and syringe to take a blood sample. She approached, all gentleness and apology, but he pulled up his jumper and said, 'Go on! Stick it in quick, so it's done before I even notice.' Near the end, when he could only speak with difficulty, I gave him some water to drink. 'Ah, some lovely water – thank you,' he said. There was something so dignified in the quiet, yet emphatic way he thanked me.

I had some lovely times with him – watching football on TV, sneaking him a little drink of port when the nurses weren't watching, and reading him stories (a poignant reminder of how, once upon a time, he read bedtime stories to me).

So I wrote this book during a significant time in my life, and that of my parents. I typed away in that little room, while the worldly winds swirled around us. Would that place in the nursing home become available for my dad? Would things go OK when the relatives visited? Would he suffer a lot of pain? Would we be able to get a message through to my brother – travelling in Africa – in time?

— —

Life is full of ups and downs, circumstances – large or small – that can trigger craving or aversion, hope or despair, longing or fear, or that can elicit from us a more creative and noble response: generosity, kindness or understanding. The Buddha often talked about these situations in terms of the eight 'worldly winds': gain and loss, fame and infamy, praise and blame, pleasure and pain.[1] In the Buddhist texts the word used is *lokadhammas*. Literally, this translates as 'worldly conditions' – the ever-changing conditions of the world, the varying circumstances of life that we will all encounter at some time or other. Some days we get what we want, other days we do not. There are times we feel loved and popular, and times when we are far from the centre of attention. On some occasions people seem to approve and praise what we do, on other occasions they criticize or censure. Sometimes life is full of pleasure or delight, but at other times pain or discomfort.

Whilst 'worldly conditions' is the literal translation, 'worldly winds' is a more poetic rendering. The metaphor of the wind is appropriate. The wind blows hither and thither, changing direction unexpectedly. We can't *see* the wind, but we feel its effects, whether it is a pleasant warm breeze or an icy, biting blast. One day storm clouds crowd the sky, the next day the wind scatters them, revealing pure, sunny blue. And it would be useless to try to stop or redirect the wind.

Likewise, the worldly winds blow back and forth. Whatever our circumstances in life, even if we are young and healthy, talented and popular, wealthy and comfortable, we'll still experience gain *and* loss, pleasure *and* pain at some time or other. The worldly winds are those circumstances in life which we cannot completely control; our only choice is in how we respond to them. Sometimes we are caught off-guard, and they blow us about, we sway and swing, our minds get into a spin. Like the wind fanning the flames of a fire, we allow the worldly winds to set the fires of craving and aversion blazing in our hearts.

They are the 'worldly' winds because they are everywhere in the world. There is no escape from them. Though they may blow in varying ways, and to different degrees, in different places, they still blow through everything: at home, at work, on holiday, at school.

These winds are 'worldly' too because to be carried along by them is to be swept along by the ways of the world. On the whole we expect the world to accord perfectly with our desires. We ignore, or try to ignore, the facts of life, the plain simple truth that life consists of complex, ever-changing conditions that we can never entirely control. On one level we know that the winds of change are blowing constantly; it sounds obvious, self-evident. And yet on some other level, deep down, we expect life to be fair, to come right. Our little irritations and disappointments, our sense of hurt and injustice when we don't get what we want, reveal this underlying delusion. Learning to sail the worldly winds involves learning when we need to give up on our desires, adjusting them to the reality of the situation. Whilst matching our desires to the world will be difficult, expecting the world to match our desires is utterly futile.

~ ~

The pages that follow contain more detailed descriptions of gain and loss, fame and infamy, praise and blame, pleasure and pain, and the myriad ways they can manifest in our lives. You'll see that some of the examples I've mentioned are very everyday; they might even seem a bit trivial. You may think: 'It's all very well talking about practising equanimity when you've stubbed your toe on the table-leg or beaten your old badminton rival seven games to nil, but what about when you're under threat of redundancy, or a family member is seriously ill?'

The reason that many of the examples given are more commonplace is precisely because they are the conditions we encounter day by day: the daily gusts and squalls, rather than a raging tornado that sweeps through our life, tossing everything up in the air. That tornado is bound to come at some point in our life; but it's the small, even trivial ups and downs of life that most of us are working with, most of the time.

Although they may be small, they are not trivial in terms of the effect they have on us. Buddhism says that actions have consequences. Everything we do or say, and the ethical intention, the mental and emotional state that motivated it, has an effect. It conditions us; it determines the kind of people we become. Looking at how we respond to the worldly winds in daily life shows us this 'karma of everyday things' – what in Buddhist tradition is called 'habitual karma'. As Buddhist teacher Sangharakshita explains:

> A very great part of one's life is probably made up of habitual karmas, things we do over and over again, often without realizing the effect they are having on us. The action may not amount to very much – it may not take up much time – but if we do it every day, perhaps several times a day, it has its effect, like drops of water wearing away a stone. All the time we are creating karma, either forging a sort of chain which binds us, or planting seeds of future growth.[2]

In terms of the worldly winds, if we notice that even small gusts and squalls can produce irritation or anxiety or complacency in us, then working on them will improve the quality of our underlying state of mind, and therefore the quality of our life. Sometimes it is these small trials of life that bring out the worst in us. It is about these that we get tetchy, anxious or small-minded. Maybe this happens because, being relatively minor, they catch us unawares. The bigger trials of life, on the other hand, can sometimes bring forth the best in us, drawing out resources of patience, kindness or perceptiveness that we hardly knew we had. Perhaps when faced with the bigger challenges of life, we are more likely to realize that circumstances are beyond our control, and that what we need to do is respond to them as creatively as we can. In those more crucial situations we can be more in touch with reality, whereas in everyday situations the illusion of control can persist. In other words, underneath those petty irritations, stubborn little attachments, persistent anxieties and all the rest, is ignorance of the nature of life. They are how our existential angst – our fear of impermanence and our desire to hold on and be in control – manifests in the everyday. There is a lot to be learned from looking at them more closely.

This book focuses on the Buddha's teaching of the worldly winds, how we can learn to navigate them more effectively, so that we can sail safely through life rather than being blown off course, however stormy the weather. It is about cultivating a more even-minded attitude to life, yet one that is still engaged, interested, concerned, and not passive or indifferent to what is happening around us. As we become more flexible and adaptable, we find a bigger perspective which helps us stay calm, even amidst the storm.

In my experience, many people find this teaching helpful, engaging and inspiring. But why? I think there are three reasons.

Firstly, it is so practical and immediate. We can each recognize the worldly winds wafting about our life. It is a simple teaching that shows the relevance of Buddhism to contemporary life and everyday events. The first chapter of the book will describe the worldly winds in more detail, and the chapter following it discusses ways to 'sail the worldly winds' – responding to them more skilfully and ethically.

Secondly, they show us the connection between ethics and wisdom. When we are swept up by the worldly winds, we are caught up unaware of the ways things are. We are trying to deny the winds of change, and are setting ourselves up for pain and disappointment. This seemingly simple teaching gets to the root of things, showing how underneath the small events that niggle at us or irritate us or mesmerize us is our desire to control and avoid. When instead we respond more skilfully and ethically, we are acting in a way that is more real and objective. Implicit or explicit in a skilful response is the recognition that we can't always control the circumstances around us.

Being aware of the worldly winds and noticing how we respond to them can help teach us 'how things are' – what Buddhists call wisdom. The third chapter explores meditation and the inner work of cultivating an even-mindedness in which such wisdom can arise. The fourth chapter of the book focuses more fully on seeing things as they really are.

A third reason I find the teaching of the worldly winds so inspiring is that it connects practice for self and for others. Buddhist practice is not just about *us* learning how to be less blown about. It is also about helping *others* find shelter in a storm. If we are blown hither and thither, we create a flurry around us, and increase the chances that others will be tossed about too. But if we can hold our course in all the winds that blow, we create calm and clarity, and that, too, may influence others, giving them the confidence and clarity not to be so thrown around. The more positive spiritual qualities we have, the more we can be a force for good in the world.

If we pay attention to the world around us, we'll see, or feel, that the worldly winds are always blowing, sometimes with a terrible force. We may know people who have lost their jobs in an economic downturn, or see pictures on TV of the devastation caused by an earthquake. The worldly winds will always blow; they are an unavoidable part of life. And their force and direction varies according to the prevailing cultural conditions. Judging by the number of times the Buddha mentioned the worldly winds, they certainly blew people around in his day, but our experience of them is probably rather different today. Chapter 5 is an attempt to explore how they bluster through our twenty-first century world, in the age of the internet, consumerism, celebrity culture and material comfort. In particular, we're going to be looking at scientism and consumerism – two myths or ideologies that are prevalent in our culture. I'll argue they contain a subtle, and often hidden, message which can nevertheless affect and condition us. They promise a world in which the worldly winds *can* be controlled, but it is a false promise. We'll be looking at how modern Buddhism needs to critique these views and offer an alternative.

— —

How to use this book

Throughout the book you'll find reflections, exercises and suggestions for practice that are designed to help you make more of the material in the book. The temptation (I know it well!) is to devour a book and get onto the next one as quickly as possible. But we need time to digest. We can tend to do six hours' reading, and maybe just an hour's reflection, but it would be better to do six hours' reflection for every hour we spend reading. We need to think about whether we agree with what is said, and how it might apply to our own life. It is that considering, thinking and wondering that reveals the gold – if you are willing to give time to it. We need to dig down into the material, sifting through it, looking for the gleam of gold. It might not come to light straight away. We have to learn to '*live* the questions' as the famous quote from Rilke puts it. 'Perhaps you will then gradually, without noticing it, live along some distant day into the answer.'[3] We sift through ever-deeper layers, finding new seams of gold.

So I'd encourage you to make use of the reflections in the book,[4] and relate the ideas and teachings you read about to the issues and challenges of your own life. The final chapter looks at some ways to create supportive conditions in our life to sustain our practice, keep it alive and engaged, so that we can respond more creatively to the worldly winds. It is designed to help you apply the material of the earlier chapters in your daily life, and to be a practical guide to sailing the worldly winds.

1

Blown by the wind

In this teaching of the worldly winds the Buddha describes the changing conditions of life that can trigger our craving or aversion, if we let them. The worldly winds consist of four pairs of opposites, as in the diagram below:

Loss	Gain
Infamy	Fame
Blame	Praise
Pain	Pleasure

We naturally tend to want to avoid those on the left-hand side, and experience more of the ones on the right-hand side. In a way, there is nothing wrong with this, as long as we remember that we will experience them *all* at some point in our lives. However, if we are too dependent on experiencing those on the right, and too determined to avoid the others, we are setting ourselves up for disappointment. We've staked our happiness on the winds blowing one way, although there are sure to be times when they blow in the other direction. When we are caught up in this way, our moods will swing with the wind. One day life's a breeze; we feel confident, lucky or happy. The next day circumstances change and we're in a spin, feeling despondent or unfairly treated by life. We oscillate between delight and dejection. Our self-view is inflated, then deflated. We veer from bewitchment to bewilderment at what life brings us. Even when we get what we long for, the pleasure may be tinged with the painful fear of losing it. We're caught in a game of opposites.

Because a lot of striving and energy can go into these tussles with the world, it may sound surprising if I suggest that this dependence on worldly conditions for our happiness is a kind of passivity. It is perhaps easier to see why this might be the case with the 'negative' worldly winds. If we don't get what we want, or experience blame, we can sometimes lose confidence or initiative, and succumb to a form of victim mentality. But the 'positive' worldly winds can also involve a kind of passivity; we are expecting something outside us to deliver happiness, expecting life to come up with the goods. And on those occasions when we do get them, we can become over-reliant on them, and this, too, entails a passive relationship to life.

Gain and loss

I used to live in a row of little terraced houses where parking could be a problem. I noticed that as I drove up my street, eager to get back home, I'd start to feel a bit anxious. I knew that quite often there would be no parking spaces left by late evening, when I was getting home. This meant I had to search the side streets for a space, and then walk back carrying my bags. It was all the more annoying because I'd noticed that the two people who lived next door to me owned *three* cars, and one of those cars was often parked outside my house. As I drove up the road a little running commentary on this would be replaying in my mind. But on those days when there was a space right near my house I'd feel almost euphoric. Surprising degrees of emotion could be generated by eight square metres of tarmac.

Small instances of gain and loss are happening all the time, so we have to deal with a constant succession of them. I'm expecting the utility bill to be big this month, but when it arrives I'm pleasantly surprised at how low it is. Maybe I can afford that new coat I wanted after all. I go shopping and am delighted with my new coat. Then I get back to the car park to discover that someone's backed into my car. I'm looking forward to a morning off work, but then my elderly mother phones, needing some help with her shopping, and I experience my free morning dissolving and disappearing into thin air. I go for an interview for a place at college and get offered a place. There are job losses in the offing at work, and the atmosphere is gossipy, anxious and edgy. I join a queue at the supermarket check-out and notice how all the other queues seem to move more quickly. How come I *always* choose the slowest queue? Then I start to bristle with indignation when the woman behind the check-out has a pleasant exchange of words with the customer in front of me. Don't they realize some people are in a hurry? Or, with just one item to buy, I join the queue, and the lady in front of me, who has a whole trolley-load, lets me go first.

We can experience the worldly winds of gain and loss in respect of possessions, relationships, money, social standing, time . . . anything which we can relate to in terms of 'that is mine', or 'I want that'. In this game of gain and loss we narrow down, our perspective shrinks. It is just me versus the world, head-down, tunnel vision, trying to get where I want, as quickly as I can get there, or what I want, as quickly as I can get it. And then there are the times when these worldly winds blow more strongly – when a child is born, or a relative passes away, when you hear that your job is on the line in a time of financial uncertainty, or learn that you will receive a large and unexpected inheritance.

Fame and infamy

Most of us won't ever experience much fame or infamy, celebrity or notoriety. But these worldly winds may still be at work if we are blown about by our desire to be popular, well-liked, or at the centre of attention. Maybe we sometimes laugh at jokes that aren't funny because we don't want to be disliked. Or we find we are not really listening to what the other person is saying; we're just waiting to jump in with our own joke, so we can be the centre of attention. Or we notice how our attitude to people at work is conditioned by whether they are liked by everyone else, and by how that popularity or unpopularity might rub off on us.

Of course there is a natural and healthy desire to be well-regarded by others, but sometimes our desire goes further and deeper than that. We have an instinctual desire to be noticed. Perhaps, in an idle moment, we find ourselves typing our own name into Google to see whether the world has registered our existence. We wonder how the number of Facebook friends we have compares to everyone else. Someone shows us some photos of a recent party, and our eyes scan over them, but what we're really interested in is how *we* look in the photos. As an author, I know the temptation, when wandering round a bookshop, to take a peek at whether *my* books are in stock.

I once wrote an article for a local newspaper in which I was a little bit provocative. In the time between sending the article off and its appearance in the newspaper, I alternated between hoping it would cause a stir and generate favourable comments, and anxiety that I'd misjudged it and would make myself unpopular. In the event, it received absolutely no response at all. This was even more galling. Sometimes, it seems, anonymity is even less desirable than infamy. I found the whole episode rather chastening.

Then there is the effect on us of the fame of others. Fame can be strangely alluring. One afternoon I was in the café of an arts centre in a small town, drinking coffee and reading a book. A few tables away I noticed a dozen or so people crowded round, a gaggle of excitement and conversation. Eventually I realized that the lady at the middle of it all had been one of the stars of a TV comedy series in the 1980s. She was in town to switch on the Christmas lights and star in the local pantomime. I primly told myself that I wasn't in the slightest bit interested in such a very minor celebrity. Yet I couldn't help glancing over. I wanted to know what she looked like, how she talked, what she'd *be like*. There is something magic and magnetic about fame. We think the famous person must *have* something, and we are fascinated to know what it is. (We'll be exploring the culture of celebrity more in chapter 5.)

Praise and blame

Once, on a Buddhist retreat for newcomers, the woman leading the retreat decided to do a small ritual each time they were in the shrine room. She simply bowed to the Buddha statue on the shrine, as a mark of respect and gratitude.

The retreat seemed to go fine; then on the last day two different people came up to the retreat-leader and gave her a note on a little piece of paper. She put them in her pockets and read them later. Pulling the first note out of her right pocket, she read, 'Thank you very much for the retreat. It has made a big difference to me. I found the way you bowed to the Buddha particularly inspiring. There was just something about it I found moving and meaningful.'

Then she pulled the other note out of her left pocket and it said, 'Thank you for leading the retreat. However, I must tell you that I'm disappointed. I thought Buddhism was free of superstition and ritual and so it was a shame to see you bowing to the Buddha. It made me feel uncomfortable and spoilt the retreat for me.'

Life is just like that. Sometimes people like what we do and they give praise and approval. Sometimes they don't like it and we receive censure and blame. Sometimes we get both praise and blame for exactly the same action! However hard we try, we will not please everyone all the time. Praise and blame become 'worldly winds' when we are blown about by them, and when our confidence or self-view is inflated or deflated, blown up or punctured, depending on which way the wind blows.

There is often a culture of blame operating in the world around us. Gossip in the workplace often consists of blaming and complaining. A lot of political discussion is likewise based on praise or blame. In England many people observe a ritual of praise and blame towards the national football team. In the build-up to a major competition there is the most unbelievable hype and hope about the team, and speculation that this time, maybe this time, they will do well. Sadly, however, the performance is often mediocre. The next day the recriminations begin, and the newspapers and websites are rife with rumours that the manager will soon be sacked.

Blame is often about control; it is where we put our disgruntlement when we don't get what we want.[5] Our frustration needs an outlet, so we find someone to blame. It must be *somebody's* fault! Blaming restores our sense of power over the world; it is a way of shoring up the illusion of control.

Recently a friend of mine needed to catch a plane to see relatives in another country. This was during the winter, when we were experiencing particularly severe snowy and icy weather. The papers and TV reports were full of horror stories about the airport and how it was virtually shut down. It was as if the snow and ice were the airport authorities' fault. But when you looked at the airport's website you could see that actually most of the flights were still operating, if somewhat delayed by the weather. If flights were badly delayed or cancelled this was often due to poor weather at the destination airport. But the media loves to find someone to blame, because reporters know that *we* want someone to blame too. All this blame will have only caused more hassle and anxiety for passengers and airport staff. The reports turned out to be hugely exaggerated, and my friend got her flight with no problems.

Nietzsche, ever-sharp, observed that 'we praise or blame according to whether the one or the other offers a greater opportunity for our power of judgement to shine out.'[6] Bearing that in mind, as well as noticing how we are affected by praise and blame when they come our way, we can also reflect on how we give out praise and blame. Of course, some praise and blame is helpful and necessary. It is good to be appreciative, to notice and acknowledge things well done; and sometimes we do need to give criticism, to point out when things have been done badly. But we can try to do this objectively and constructively, not criticizing as an outlet for our frustration, or praising from our desire to ingratiate ourselves.

Pleasure and pain

You're hyper-excited, as you're going on holiday tomorrow. Or a toothache makes you moody. You are making a cup of tea and find there's no milk in the fridge, and you find yourself feeling exasperated. You come out of the gym with a spring in your step. Or you've been relentlessly busy and your shoulders are coiled tight. Your spirits lift when the sun comes out. Or you get annoyed, as you're stuck in a traffic jam in hot weather, and inside the car it is stifling. You feel bright and breezy as today you're going on an outing which you know you'll enjoy. Or there's a chore that you've been putting off for weeks, as you think it will be 'a real pain'. But it must be done today and so you feel a bit gloomy and grumpy.

As well as those minor kinds of discomforts and inconveniences, there are times in life when the worldly winds blow more strongly.

There will be moments of exquisite pleasure, when everything seems perfect. But as we get older we will also notice more aches and pains in the body. Many people start to suffer chronic pain, and most of us will have to face serious illness at some time or other.

It's not that it's wrong to enjoy pleasure when it comes, or avoid pain where possible. It is just that you can't control your experience all the time. Observing these particular worldly winds is about noticing how even minor comforts or discomforts can swing our mood, because we cling on to comforts and try to perpetuate them, and resist discomforts and make them worse than they need to be. We'll be exploring more how this happens in the next chapter.

Reflection: blown by the wind?

There are lots of ways to reflect – maybe you already have your own method for reflection. But if not, here is one suggestion. Firstly, you need time to sit quietly, so that busy thoughts can settle, and more considered thoughts can arise. Have a pencil and paper and jot down ideas, observations and memories as they occur to you. Do you recognize the worldly winds blowing in your life? Try to recall small or large instances of the winds that have blown you around in the last few days. Then maybe think about patterns or themes that tend to loom large or recur often in your life. You can write a list, or you can do one of those spidery diagrams. It doesn't matter which, the point is to get the ideas down. Writing, rather than just thinking about them, helps tease them out. When you've got to put your reflections on paper, it helps make them more clear and objective.

Are there particular worldly winds that blow around you more frequently than others? Or are there some that tend to affect you more strongly? Or are there certain kinds of situation in which you are more susceptible to being blown around?

Try to pay attention to both directions – in other words, how you may be affected by pleasure as well as pain, gain as well as loss. Often it is easier to notice when the worldly winds are blowing in the 'negative' direction, and we just don't notice our response when they blow the other way.

Are there other varying circumstances of life that don't quite seem to fit into the traditional formulation? What are they? (For example, a friend of mine realized he was influenced by desire for success and fear of failure. They were 'worldly winds' for him.)

2

Learning to sail
the worldly winds

Now that we have identified the worldly winds and how they may blow in our lives, this chapter looks at how to respond to them. How might we be less buffeted about and learn, eventually, to rise above them, sailing the winds of change more skilfully? We're going to look at four stages of practice:

1) Recognize the worldly winds.
2) Distinguish control from influence.
3) See the worldly winds as opportunities.
4) Listen to the stories we tell.

As we go along there will also be suggested reflections, exercises, and suggestions for your daily practice. Also, in the last chapter, there are more ideas for practice in everyday life, particularly on how to 'remember to remember' our aspirations and intentions whilst we're in the thick of it.

1) Recognize the worldly winds

This means simply looking out for the worldly winds, being aware of them, noticing the times and situations when they are more likely to blow us about. Once we bear them in mind in the midst of daily life, we may start noticing more and more instances of them. The teaching of the worldly winds becomes a helpful way in which we can look at our daily experience and see what is really going on.

Just that act of noticing has an effect. We're starting to create awareness, a space or a pause between what happens to us and our response. You could even see the worldly winds as like little demons; just naming them and being aware of them gives you more power over them. (This is a traditional Buddhist approach to dealing with the 'demons' that beset us.)

2) Distinguish control from influence

Having spotted we're in the midst of a situation in which the worldly winds are blowing, we can think about what is happening in terms of control and influence. Ask yourself to what extent what is happening is really under your control. Or is it outside your control? Do you need to change and adapt? Can you respond to the situation in a way that will have a helpful influence on your state of mind, and, if possible, on the situation around you? In other words, what is a 'given' in the situation, and what is a 'possible'? What we can't control, we just have to accept. When there is something we *can* influence, well, let's try to do what we can.

A loved one is in hospital, seriously ill, and you are waiting for them to be transferred to a specialist ward. It is so urgent and important to you, and yet it depends on factors – the busyness of the hospital staff, the availability of a bed in the new ward – which are entirely outside your control. This lack of control is likely to cause us stress and anxiety if we don't recognize and work with it. But maybe there are small ways in which you can have a helpful influence: speaking calmly to the hospital staff to ensure the issue is on their radar, and telling the patient and other relatives the objective facts of the situation.

Or you're on your way to the airport to catch a flight and your train has been cancelled. Again, the situation is outside your control, but how you respond will influence your state of mind and that of others around you. A calmer response will lead to more presence of mind, which may lead you to remembering that you've got a friend who is off work this week, and that means he might be able to give you a lift . . .

There is a well-known story of a Zen master who was flying back home after visiting his disciples in a foreign country. He and one of his students, who was escorting him to the airport, were waiting for the bus, but it hadn't turned up. The student was anxious, pacing up and down the pavement, making panicky calls on her mobile phone. At one point she looked across at the Zen teacher. He was just sitting on his suitcase, enjoying the sunshine. She realized that not only was he not worried, he wasn't even *waiting*. He knew there was nothing to be done, and could drop all desire to control the situation, and, instead, simply sit in the sun.

Of course, accepting things that are outside our control, giving up on wishing something will go one way, and letting go of our frustration because it has gone the other, is not always easy. Sometimes the emotions at play are strong. But the first task is to recognize more clearly the situation we are in, to bring more awareness in. Knowing the nature of the worldly winds and distinguishing between control and influence may help us do that. It is a kind of stepping back into a broader perspective. From this perspective we may be able to see other possibilities that just weren't apparent to us when we were caught up in the situation.

Reflection: control and influence

Looking back at the reflection at the end of the last chapter on how the worldly winds tend to blow in your life, can you see how you might resist those situations, trying to retain the illusion of control? How does that manifest? What does it feel like? What would it feel like to be able to give up control and just do what you can to have a positive influence?

It might help to close your eyes, relax for a few minutes, and then imagine yourself in some of those situations. Reflecting in this way may help you to connect with how it felt, and to recall the kinds of thoughts that were going on. It may also enable you to imagine a different kind of response, and what that would look and feel like.

3) See the worldly winds as opportunities

Next, some suggestions as to how we might influence the situation for the better, for ourselves and for those around us. Rather than reacting and just trying to swing back from loss to gain, or from blame to praise, and so on, we try to respond with awareness of the worldly winds. We can try to turn those swings back and forth into spiritual opportunities. If we've allowed our mood or self-view to be swayed by them, this is our chance to regain the initiative. Rather than hoping or expecting that the world will give us what we want all the time, we look at what we can bring to the situation. We see the worldly winds as teachers, spurring us on to develop patience, courage, or whatever response the situation calls for. We welcome the challenge, relish the chance to grow. Just having this attitude, bringing it to mind, remembering it in the thick of things, already makes a difference. We've regained the initiative. We've found a way to engage meaningfully and creatively with our circumstances. We may begin to feel quite differently about the situation we're in.

Another image to describe this is that we look for 'Dharma-doors'. We can get caught in a game of opposites, dualities, fearing one thing, longing for its opposite. We're trapped in this game if we see *only* opposites, and no other possibility, no way of playing it differently. But if we look at the situation as a spiritual opportunity, we may discern some new quality that we can bring in. This new quality is like a Dharma-door, giving us a way out of the trap of opposites. (The word 'Dharma' means a path, teaching, or truth that leads towards Enlightenment, and so these are the doors through which we can head in the right direction.)

Here are some suggestions for turning the worldly winds into opportunities, or for finding those Dharma-doors. For each pair of worldly winds, we're also going to look at some stories from the Buddha's life, stories that show him navigating them skilfully.

a) From gain and loss into generosity

We'll be buffeted by gain and loss if we relate to the world as a struggle to get what we want. A radically different strategy to take, a way to turn the rules on their head and play the game differently, is to practise generosity, to try to relate to the world on the basis of 'what I can give' rather than 'what I can get'.

We can try this in an area of life that we all have to deal with sometimes, and some of us cope with every day: driving or cycling in busy traffic, or walking through crowded streets. Instead of getting annoyed with the man who suddenly switches lane and swerves right in front of us, or the woman who is standing oblivious at the top of the subway answering her mobile phone while commuters mutter and try to squeeze past her, we can try to be generous in our attitude and in our response. Maybe we can slow down and let a few cars out of that awkward junction. Or instead of pushing past the woman on the stairs, we can gently but firmly say something to help bring her back into awareness. We might arrive home two minutes later, but we will be in a much better frame of mind. Who knows, those other people might be in a slightly better mood too.

Driving, cycling or walking through a busy city is like a mirror to your state of mind. If you are not in such a good state, you may notice the journey is stop/start/stop/start: you proceed abruptly, jumpily, pushily, tetchily. When you are in a good state you can navigate busy situations with much more awareness and therefore much more 'flow' and smoothness of travel. Maybe you can turn this into a deliberate practice: the tai chi of traffic!

～～

The Buddhist text that tells the story of the Buddha's last months and days, his death and attainment of *parinibbāna* (final, complete, nirvana) is, interestingly, the longest *sutta* (discourse) in the early Buddhist scriptures.[7] No doubt the Buddha's last days were especially significant to his followers; the way he approached death was a teaching for them. Certainly there are incidents that show the Buddha rising above gain and loss and practising unstinting generosity. The sutta describes moments of love and friendship that are very human and poignant. At the same time, something different about the Buddha shines through: the completeness of his equanimity and his lack of concern with the ways of the world.

The Buddha knows he is dying. His once healthy body is now old and frail. It is, as he himself puts it, like 'an old cart . . . held together with straps'.[8] He goes on a final tour with Ānanda, his long-time friend and closest companion. They visit old haunts, places of natural beauty, shrines and woodland groves. These are places they have passed through many times before, and the Buddha knows he will not see them again. He looks on them with loving eyes for one last time.

At another time the Buddha mourns Śāriputra and Maudgalyāyana, two of his foremost disciples, who have recently died. They and the Buddha would have lived, worked and travelled together over many years; they had been brothers together in their task of establishing the sangha (the Buddhist community). And now Śāriputra and Maudgalyāyana were gone. The Buddha declares:

> The assembly seems empty to me now that Śāriputra and Maudgalyāyana have attained final nirvana . . . It is impossible that what is born and subject to disintegration should not disintegrate; and yet, it is as if the largest branches have broken off a great tree.[9]

You sense that the Buddha misses them, though he does not let this lead him into denying the reality of life and death. He looks loss in the eye, calmly and directly, but not without a tenderness that is very human.

Though he is sick and weak, afflicted with 'sharp and deadly pains', he constantly thinks of others, and gives to them. There is the oft-quoted story in which Ānanda, knowing the Buddha will soon die, is overcome by grief, distraught and weeping. The Buddha is firm and challenging, reminding Ānanda, 'Have I not already told you that all things that are pleasant and delightful are changeable, subject to separation . . . How could it be that it should not pass away?'[10] But he is also kind and gentle, rejoicing in Ānanda's qualities and expressing gratitude for the way he has looked after him for many years.

There is a smith named Cunda who has served the Buddha a meal, but it has given him food poisoning. Cunda is full of remorse and regret. The Buddha notices this and asks Ānanda to make sure everyone knows that offering the Buddha his last ever meal is a highly auspicious and worthy thing to do. He sees that Cunda prepared the meal with good intentions, and so there is no cause for him to feel remorse. He also knows that there might be whisperings of blame amongst his followers, so he gives praise and gratitude instead. He acts to ensure that the worldly winds of blame do not blow unnecessarily around Cunda.

Then, when the Buddha is on his death-bed in a grove of *sāl* trees, a wanderer comes by who wants to meet him. Ānanda wants the Buddha, who is now very weak, to be left in peace,

and asks Subhadda the wanderer to go away. But the Buddha
calls him back and talks to him, and Subhadda becomes the last
ever personal disciple of the Buddha. Even in his last minutes, the
Buddha sailed above gain and loss, and was ready to give.

b) From fame and infamy into individuality

Now we are going to look at how to steer a course through the
worldly winds of 'fame and infamy'. Again, in the text that
describes the Buddha's last weeks there are some incidents in
which these worldly winds are blowing and we see how the
Buddha dealt with them.

At one point Ānanda and the Buddha, on their final visits to
people and places, end up in a small town called Kuśinagara.
Here the Buddha decides he will spend his final days. 'But why
die here?' asks Ānanda, 'in this miserable little town of wattle-
and-daub, right in the jungle in the back of beyond?'[11] Ānanda is
clearly thinking that it would be more fitting for the Buddha's last
hours to be spent in one of the great and grand cities thereabouts.
But the Buddha tells Ānanda not to be rude about Kuśinagara,
saying that it was once a great city, bustling and prosperous, and
the headquarters of an even bigger empire.

What is the significance of this episode? One interpretation[12]
is that the Buddha is hinting at the growth and decline of worldly
things. The wheel of fortune never stops turning; what once rose
to prominence will eventually fall into obscurity again. He is
pointing out to Ānanda that to die in a grand place is not really
very meaningful.

They've just heard that an old friend and patron, King
Pasenadi, has been cruelly deposed, and has died of fatigue
outside the gates of a nearby city. There is other political turmoil in
the region, including war against the Buddha's and Ānanda's own
people, the Śākyans. Members of their own families have recently
been murdered. And on their way here, they've seen a fortress

being built at Pāṭaligāma by another tribe, the Magadhans, who are preparing for war against their neighbours, the Vajjians. The Buddha tried to intervene to prevent war, but he sensed that he had not, that time, met with success. What they were witnessing, he realized, was the start of a new empire, whose chief city would be based round that fortress.

Even in the circle of his own followers, the sangha – now larger, more dispersed – the Buddha is a less influential figure. He is older and has less energy with which to intervene. It is as if the Buddha is saying, 'All this is just the way of the world. Let us not conduct our affairs on the world's terms. Let us especially not worry about making a spectacle, about fame and repute. Let us just do what we can to pass on the Dharma.'

That is what the Buddha *is* concerned with: his legacy and his teaching of the Dharma. It is not as if his unworldly attitude is a world-weary sigh of 'Oh, I can't be bothered.' He *is* bothered about the reputation of the Dharma, especially after he is gone. On this farewell tour he has met many of his followers and always he has asked them if they have any last questions. He checks with them again and again. Soon, he tells them, he will be gone and they will have to be 'islands unto themselves', so they should clear up any doubts and uncertainties while he is still there. He gives instructions for his funeral and advises on pilgrimage places of the future.

There are records of many occasions when the Buddha warned his followers against the dangers of being taken in by fame, honour and esteem.[13] That should never be their motive for living the spiritual life. The sense is of a man 'in the world, but not of the world'. He is unaffected by worldly values, by personal gain or fame, but he is not other-worldly in the sense of being impractical or unconcerned about his legacy and its potential to benefit others.

So perhaps it is through individuality that we avoid being rocked by the worldly winds of fame and infamy. Individuality includes integrity and wholeness; possessing it, we have a sense of who we are and what our values and priorities are, and we try to act in accordance with them. It is allied with a range of other qualities: the awareness to know ourselves, truthfulness, the courage to be ourselves even if it means going against the grain of popular opinion. This, of course, can be far from easy.

Individuality must be distinguished from individual*ism*. Individualism is pushing through the world, always asserting oneself over and above that world. It often doesn't manifest very crudely or obviously, but individualism is the attitude that life is about getting what I want. I won't necessarily take account of the individuality of others; my relationships will tend to be based on what suits what I want.

By contrast, *mettā*, or loving-kindness, is an awareness and affirmation of the being of another person.[14] In other words, it's one individual human being becoming aware of another. When we are being more individual, our sense of value and worth comes from our inner values, and also from our relationships with people we love and who love us, and want to support our individuality. Our sense of worth doesn't come from without, from worldly values, or from how we are seen in the eyes of the world. Being an individual doesn't mean we can't change or adapt our beliefs or opinions as a result of discussion with other people, but we won't change them simply in order to fit in.

Sometimes, when people are disapproving of us or upset with us, we just have to learn not to take it personally. We're not going to be able to please everyone all the time. We need to ask ourselves whether we said what we believe to be true, and whether we did that with a good and kind motive. After that, it is up to other people how they respond. We can't be over-responsible for their reactions. We learn to rely on what we believe to be true, whilst being willing to modify our position in the light of experience.

Apparently, from the time of the Renaissance in Italy to the First World War, hundreds of thousands of young men lost their lives in duels. Often the challenge to a duel was prompted by a trivial incident, but one which was perceived as a slight to 'honour'.[15] Perhaps the contemporary equivalent is gang-fights in cities. I once knew someone who worked in the casualty department of a big city hospital. He explained how if young men got injured in gang-fights, the police and emergency services had to be very careful to ensure they took members of rival gangs to different hospitals. Otherwise more gang members would turn up, and the fighting would continue in the corridors of the hospital. Again, these fights would start over trivial matters, but 'honour' needed to be restored.

How do we understand such behaviour? It is a tragic case of individuality being so weak that other people's opinions are the *only* factor in forming a sense of self.[16] The challenger to the fight needs to prove they are bigger than the other person, because they feel small. Underneath the puffing and posturing is a fragile ego. It is so fragile that honour and being seen to be unafraid become the biggest values, even at risk of life or injury. They can't bear to be seen as afraid of anyone else, to be seen as a loser.

Perhaps these are extreme versions of a tendency we can recognize in ourselves. Say someone pushes in front of me in a queue, in front of lots of other people. How do I feel? Sometimes I can be prone to take offence, to feel affronted. And if I look closely and honestly at what is going on, it is not being one place back in the queue that really bothers me. It is more a question of pride, that maybe people saw someone 'get one over me'. In my desire to restore honour I blurt out a rude remark.

How do we develop individuality? It requires that we keep

asking ourselves what is most important in our lives, what we really believe in, and how we can live by that. Also, the more we develop qualities like mindfulness and *mettā* (loving-kindness), the more individual we become, having a healthy sense of ourselves that is not over-dependent on the views of others.

Such individuality is hard won; it is a lifetime's project. I remember seeing an exhibition of the work of J.M.W. Turner, perhaps England's greatest painter. He was a prolific artist and there were hundreds of paintings on show. The exhibition was arranged chronologically, so it started with early works in which you saw him absorbing all sorts of influences (that of classical landscape painters like Claude Lorraine, or of the Dutch sea-painters, for example). In the middle of the exhibition he had definitely begun to develop his own distinctive style. By the end of the exhibition the canvases were more spare and simple, and yet they conveyed so much. It was as though he had spent a whole, long, ceaselessly productive life observing the sea, rivers, trees, the sky and clouds, and, above all, the light of the sun, and he became more and more able to convey these things with seemingly less on the canvas. It is as if he spent a whole life refining his vision, his unique way of seeing the world. We could see *our* lives like that too: as a process of constantly refining a vision, and trying to express it more simply and perfectly.

c) From praise and blame into truthfulness

Next, how do we respond to the winds of praise and blame? I'm going to suggest that truthfulness is the Dharma-door through which we can enter into a greater equanimity. If we are on the receiving end of praise and blame, we can try to reflect on what is true in the situation. When praised, what can we learn about ourselves, about how others see us, about what they appreciate in us? Similarly, what can we learn from criticism, even if we don't feel it was expressed as kindly as it could have been?

Let us accept genuine appreciation and praise in a good spirit. Often our tendency can be to deny and deflect what has been said. Someone praises the essay we wrote for college and we say, 'Oh, it was just a few ideas I pinched out of a book I found in the library. It wasn't as good as that essay you wrote last week, that was really great.' It is a shame to respond like this, and thereby block someone else's appreciation and positivity. At other times we can let praise go to our heads. We get a bit intoxicated by it, start to feel we're invincible. So, let us just accept appreciation, take it in and be grateful for it. We can also give appreciation, through what Buddhists sometimes call 'rejoicing in merits'. We draw out what it is that we've noticed about the other person, what they've done well, and the effect it has had on us, or on other people. When you hear someone do this well, it can be very uplifting. They are able to be really observant of the person they are rejoicing in. What they say is not sentimental or over-blown, but accurate, really capturing a person's qualities. The more truthful the rejoicing is, the more effective and inspiring it can be.

In the last chapter we explored how blame can often be an expression of frustration when things don't go our way. Maybe, when we have a tendency to blame in this kind of way, we can instead reflect on what is true, and try to be more balanced and objective. Sometimes we *do* need to give criticism, but it will be more helpful and effective if it is accurate, and given in the right spirit.

At other times we don't know what the truth is. Something happens that inconveniences us, but we can't tell why it happened. On these occasions we should give the benefit of the doubt, until we've got a good, objective reason not to. For example, a friend of mine once walked into the shrine room on a large retreat attended by a few hundred people. He went up to where he had left his own mat and cushions and they weren't there. There were mats and cushions everywhere, but not his. Irritation started arising, and a little voice in his head started to say, 'Some blighter has pinched my cushions.' But then he caught himself, and another voice pitched in, this time giving the benefit of the doubt. 'Somebody must have known they were mine and has borrowed them because they needed them for something that was happening elsewhere.' He didn't yet know for sure, but that was a much better interim position to hold. It gave more peace of mind, and was a more trusting and positive assumption to make about the other people on retreat.

There's a story from the Buddha's life which shows how he responded to the worldly winds of praise and blame with the quality of truthfulness.[17]

In the days of the Buddha there was a whole movement of people leaving their homes and living a wandering life in search of spiritual liberation. These people were known as *śramaṇas* ('strivers'). It was a way of life accepted, even respected, by the society of that time, and the *śramaṇas* lived on donations given by the people of the towns and villages. It was this way of life that Gautama (as the Buddha was known before his Enlightenment) followed when he first embarked on his spiritual quest. Then, after he gained Enlightenment, and became the Buddha, he taught others and founded a sangha (spiritual community). Some of the sangha lived as lay people, but many also became *śramaṇas*, wandering from town to village, begging for food each morning, and settling on the outskirts of the town during the rainy season.

In this way, there was a section of society that had stepped out of conventional life, living simply, somewhat on the edge, and reliant for their survival on what the locals would give them. No doubt some of the sects and groups of wanderers were more popular with the locals, and therefore received more food and support. There's a little stock phrase that often crops up in the early Buddhist texts describing how a wanderer who was well-supported was, 'esteemed, honoured, thought much of, worshipped, he had deference paid to him, and got supplies of robes and alms food, bed and lodging, comforts and medicines for sickness.'[18]

The followers of the Buddha tended to be well respected by the locals and therefore well supported in this way. This could create friction with other sects and schools of wanderers. Sometimes the Buddha even intervened to ensure that a wealthy patron, perhaps about to begin following the Buddha's teaching, wouldn't leave those he had previously supported without any means of sustenance.

However, there were still tensions and resentments, and amongst one set of wanderers these had grown dark and bitter. They hatched a plot to discredit the Buddha's disciples. Amongst these wanderers was a beautiful young woman named Sundarī. She was an idealistic young woman, dedicated to the spiritual life, and she regarded them like brothers. She'd do anything they asked. So, they asked her to go 'oft and oft' to the Jeta Grove, which was a park donated by a wealthy patron of the Buddha, where the Buddha's homeless disciples lived, especially during the rainy season. Sundarī couldn't quite understand why she was being given such a request, it was slightly odd, but she did what she was asked. For the next few weeks she was often to be seen at the Jeta Grove, talking with people there, walking about, coming and going.

Then, one night, the plotters murdered Sundarī and buried her body in the Jeta Grove. The next day they went to King Pasenadi and slyly mentioned that Sundarī was nowhere to be seen. 'Then where might she be?' asked the king. They all shrugged their shoulders and looked blank. But then one of the attendants, standing nearby, spoke up. 'I've seen her hanging about the Jeta

Grove quite a lot recently,' he said. 'Then search the Jeta Grove,' said the king. The plotters exchanged malicious glances; their plan was falling into place.

They 'searched' the Jeta Grove and of course they 'found' Sundarī's body. Cynically they put it on a stretcher and carried it back through town, so as many people as possible would see what had happened. To everyone who looked, the plotters said, 'See, those followers of the Buddha call themselves holy, but we found poor Sundarī in the Jeta Grove.'

No doubt this caused great consternation amongst the local people. The Buddha's disciples, once so respected, were now reviled by sections of the population. Eventually things got so bad that they went to the Buddha and asked him what they should do. Of course the Buddha saw what had happened, and saw the tragedy of it for poor Sundarī. But he remained steadfast and declared that after seven days the abuse would have died down. He instructed the monks and nuns to calmly but firmly deny involvement in the crime, and to explain to people that they spoke with an underlying conviction that untruthful speech brought only misery and suffering in the future, and they would therefore only speak the truth.

His disciples did as suggested. Their calm but firm rejection of all accusations gradually had an impact on the townspeople. They were impressed by the way the Buddha's followers spoke, and the fact that they spoke on oath. Within seven days the rumours and accusations had died away. A storm of blame was abated through truthfulness. [19]

d) From pleasure and pain into mindfulness

Before his Enlightenment, Gautama had known both worlds of pleasure and worlds of pain. The legendary account of his life describes his upbringing in great material comfort. He ate fine food, was entertained by dancers and musicians, strolled round beautiful pleasure-gardens, and hunted with friends in the nearby forests. Later in life, describing it to his disciples, he said:

> I was delicate, most delicate, supremely delicate. Lily pools were made for me at my father's house solely for my benefit. Blue lilies flowered in one, white lilies in another, red lilies in a third. I used no sandalwood that was not from Benares. My turban, tunic, lower garments and cloak were all made of Benares cloth. A white sunshade was held over me day and night so that no cold or heat or dust or grit or dew might inconvenience me.[20]

But he saw through it, saw how this heavenly world – fine and beautiful though it was – was shot through with impermanence and would one day come to an end. A life in pursuit of pleasure was futile; it was a chase in which you eventually lost track of that which was desired. So where was lasting satisfaction to be found?

Deeply troubled by such questions, Gautama left home, living in the forests, joining other bands of truth-seekers, trying their way of practising. Some of them believed that liberation came by burning up all one's karma, so that one no longer needed to be reborn. And the way to rid oneself of karma was not to act, not to do anything that would generate more karma. Furthermore, the old karma could be extinguished more quickly by practising austerities – denying pleasure and seeking pain. This was the creed followed by those wanderers. Some refused to take food, except the minimum required for sustenance. Some meditated whilst sitting between burning fires. Some refused to sit or lie, and stood for days, weeks, months, even years, even sleeping on their feet. It was strange, extreme, but fuelled by a burning desire to be done with the world of oscillation between pleasure and pain.

And so Gautama tried this way too. His determination being so firm, he pushed it harder, went closer to the edge than anyone before him. But it didn't work. He saw that although his body got weaker, he was no nearer liberation. However wilfully he strove, his mind eventually returned to craving pleasure. There was no real freedom from the duality of pleasure and pain.

He started eating proper food again, to regain strength. Some ascetic friends thought he'd given up on the quest, and abandoned him. He was left all alone. It was a moment of deep crisis. He'd given up so much in leaving his luxurious palace. Now, some years of struggle later, he'd tried all the teachings on offer and he'd got no further than when he had just left home.

Then, a memory from long ago came back to him,[21] and he intuitively knew it contained a valuable clue to his search. The memory was of a day in his childhood when he had been taken out to see the fields being ploughed for the new season. He was sitting under a rose-apple tree, which was full of delicate, pale blossom. The sun shone, sunlight sparkled in the fresh green leaves, and the birds were singing at their fullest. It was a lovely scene, full of hope and anticipation of the coming spring, and all this beauty transported the little boy.

But then he became aware of another aspect of what lay before his eyes. The men who ploughed the field were bent double, their backs straining, their limbs sweating, their faces creased and wrinkled by years of working in the harsh sun. The cattle that dragged the plough strained their bodies, with a look of dead resignation in their eyes. As hard as they pulled, they only received more prods and blows from the sticks of the men. As the blade of the plough turned over the earth, the boy could see insects scrambling and worms wriggling, their little world turned upside down. Birds flew down, dodging the heavy feet of the cattle, squabbling between themselves and gobbling up the insects.

Maybe, in his imagination, the little boy could see even more than this. Perhaps he knew that the fields had been jungle only a few years before. In his mind's eye, he could see men clearing the forest, burning the trees and hacking at the undergrowth to make more land for growing crops. He could see birds fleeing their nests in confusion. He saw monkeys leaping from branches and shrieking as the trees fell.

In other words, he saw the suffering that was inherent in life. He saw life as a struggle: animals had to fight for survival, but humans also struggled constantly against nature. It was unavoidable, and, seeing this, there welled up in him a deep compassion. Naturally and spontaneously, this lifted him into a meditative state.

Now, years later, he reflected on what had happened under that rose-apple tree, and much valuable understanding and insight arose out of this memory. It was an experience of the beauty and pleasure of life. But it was also an experience of how, woven into that, is pain and suffering. This led to a welling up of compassion, and hinted to him that it was through understanding and compassion that liberation was really to be found. It also taught him that wilfully entering meditative states, as he'd learned to do, would not work. Instead, there was a more natural, integrated way in which the process of meditation could unfold.

The memory of the rose-apple tree helped him to see how to relate to pleasure and pain. Formerly he had sought pleasure; latterly he had become frightened of it, and felt he needed to shun it. But now he saw that pleasure and pain were not inherently good or bad in themselves. Later, after his Enlightenment, and having now developed his teaching, the Buddha expressed it thus:

> There are two kinds of happiness: the kind to be pursued and the kind to be avoided . . . When I observed that in the pursuit of such happiness, unwholesome factors increased and wholesome factors decreased, then that happiness was to be avoided. And when I observed that in the pursuit of such happiness unwholesome factors decreased and wholesome ones increased, then that happiness was to be sought after.[22]

He said that the same was true of sadness and non-pleasure; the same was even true of equanimity. In other words, feelings are not good or bad, right or wrong, in themselves. You have to see where they are leading you, and what their effect is. To a smoker, a cigarette seems pleasurable, but it is actually leading to harm. To a child, medicine seems horrid, but it may be doing them good. If you have spoken unkindly to someone, you may feel remorse, and this is painful, but it may spur you to apologize and redeem the situation. It is important to experience our feelings, but in order to know what they are telling us, we need to look more deeply at them, and not only at whether they are pleasant or painful. Feelings on their own do not always tell the truth.

The Buddha once gave a teaching called the 'Two Arrows'.[23] He said that inevitably we will sometimes experience pain and discomfort, and often what we do is resist that pain, or worry about it, or complain, or feel bitter, and so on. In other words, to an experience of physical pain we add a further layer of mental and emotional pain. This second layer of pain is added by us; it is not inevitable. The Buddha said it is as if we have been hit by an arrow, but then we fire a second arrow into ourselves.

The resistance and all the mental and emotional activity involved in it is essentially a kind of focusing of energy around the painful experience. This may make the pain worse, or make it feel worse. For example, sometimes when resisting bodily discomfort, our body can tense up, and eventually that can make our body feel even more painful.

What happens next in this process of resistance, says the Buddha, is that we try to avoid the pain by finding some distraction. We look for something – anything – which will give us some degree of pleasure and take our mind off the pain. We think that the only way to escape from pain is to block it off with some other kind of experience. Those distractions may take many different forms: watching hours of TV, smoking, talking non-stop, or tidying your office for the fifth time that day. It is a desperate strategy of trying to swing from pain back to pleasure. Vidyamala, a Buddhist practitioner who works with people suffering from chronic pain, describes it vividly:

> When I first heard this I didn't agree as my main response to pain is to push things away, rather than seeking pleasure to replace it. Instead of reaching for the chocolates, I'm more likely to pick a fight. But on deeper reflection I realized I was picking fights because, perverse though it might be, I found having an argument more enjoyable than experiencing the pain . . .
>
> . . . As well as arguing I find myself restlessly surfing the Internet, wandering round the house like a caged animal, making myself endless cups of tea and finding myself surveying the contents of the fridge without quite knowing how I got there. All these states are accompanied by tension and strain and it can be a tremendous effort to stop whatever I'm doing and come back to a more whole and aware experience of myself.[24]

It becomes progressively harder to turn back to our experience because distraction becomes more and more of a habit. Moreover, within the world of distraction, our experience becomes more shallow, more unsatisfying and therefore more painful, and so then it seems even harder to turn back to that experience.

This can become a painful state of existence. It is like being a monkey running away from something that is tied to his tail. He runs and runs, but when he stops and looks back, he sees that it is still there, and starts running again. These displacement activities tend to be tiring and stressful *because* they involve running away from, rather than turning towards, our experience. Paradoxically, we're putting more energy into what we're trying to escape from. It is only through awareness, through finding out what is going on, looking at our experience more fully and deeply, that we connect with the energy that is bound up with and involved in the pain and avoidance, and then we can find relaxation.

This doesn't mean it's never OK to distract yourself. If you suffer from pain you might decide to do something pleasurable, treat yourself, as a way of taking your mind off the pain for a while. But this is a mindful, conscious strategy. It is an aware choice, not habitual denial and resistance, not trying to block off and push away.

The metaphor of an arrow is a strong one. You can inflict a lot of harm with an arrow. Likewise, you can inflict a lot of unnecessary harm with your mind. Think of all the worries you carry in your mind about things that are never going to happen. Think of all the assumptions you've made about people, and the irritation you've borne towards them, only to find out that your assumption was wrong. Think of all the energy you've invested in wishing something that is just a fact of life will go away. It all adds up to a lot of unnecessary suffering. Sometimes we stumble around, unaware, clutching onto our bows and arrows – a dangerous scenario.

Vidyamala, quoted above, has founded an organization called Breathworks[25] which teaches mindfulness to help people suffering from chronic pain due to illness or injury. She says that resistance to pain can be the major cause of people's pain and distress. Mindfulness may not take all the pain away, but it can help bring about a changed relationship with that pain, an acceptance of it which brings relief and takes away much of the strain and distress.

We may not suffer from chronic pain, but we may still be shooting ourselves in the foot with that second arrow. We get irritable when it is too hot and stuffy, or when a young child is screaming noisily in our favourite café, or when the supermarket has run out of the food item we want.

So the practice of mindfulness is the way to course through the worldly winds of pleasure and pain. In the case of pain, it's a case of working with it rather than fighting it. When painful experiences occur, try to remain mindful. Try not to add the second arrow of resistance or irritation, or any of the other forms of craving and aversion, try not to deny the experience, but accept what has happened, or is happening. Of course this doesn't mean we shouldn't avoid or relieve the pain if that is possible.

So far this section has been about painful experience, but the parable of the arrow can apply to pleasurable experience too. When a pleasant experience comes your way, the aim is to enjoy it, but without being intoxicated by it and starting to crave its continuance. Sometimes when we're enjoying something, there's a thought at the back of our mind about when we'll next be able to do the same thing again. Or, sitting in the cinema enjoying a film, we start to wonder whether it might have been even more enjoyable to have watched something else. This longing and wondering is also a kind of second arrow, which removes us from the enjoyment of the present.

The Buddha practised all this himself. Towards the end of his life when he was sick and suffering 'sharp pains as if he were about to die', the suttas tell us he 'endured all this mindfully and clearly aware, and without complaint.'[26] He felt it, he didn't block it off, but nor did it lead him into negative mental states. There was no second arrow.

Although the simple wandering life was frugal, and in some ways hard, you sense there was pleasure in it too. The Buddha appreciated its simplicity, he enjoyed natural beauty, and he could dwell in the pleasure of inspired and expansive states of meditation. Sometimes the early texts describe the Buddha slipping away from the crowds and going into the forests to meditate. He spent much of his life on the road, working for others, but he also found time for restorative, healthy enjoyment.

— —

Reflection: sailing with the worldly winds – seeing the worldly winds as opportunities

Go back to your notes about the reflection at the end of chapter 1, where you looked at how the worldly winds blow in your life. Now reflect on whether there are ways you could turn these situations into opportunities. Could the worldly winds become spiritual teachers? Or, to change the image, what would be the 'Dharma-doors', the qualities that you could bring into play, that would stop you swinging between opposites, and help you rise above them?

- *Are there ways you could respond with generosity to times of gain and loss?*
- *Can you see instances in your life in which you could meet fame and infamy with individuality?*
- *How might you practise truthfulness when the worldly winds of praise and blame are blowing around you?*
- *Can you see opportunities to bring mindfulness into situations of pleasure and pain?*

The qualities, or 'Dharma-doors', that I have talked about above are only some possible suggestions. You may think of others that are appropriate to your situation.

You might do this sitting quietly with pen and paper, like in the first reflection. Or another approach might be to sit in meditation. Imagine yourself in a situation in which you can tend to get blown about, and then try to see, or feel, how you would deal with it if you were at your very best. Or maybe think about how someone you admire would respond, or even what the Buddha would do in that situation. This may take time, so don't worry if 'answers' do not come straight away.

Reflect on the above with respect to the four pairs of worldly winds. Then choose just one pair to work with, to try to put into practice, in the coming week. (I suggest only one, since it is best not to take on too much at once.) At the end of the week, assess how you got on. Was it easy to remember it when you were in the thick of it? And did it make any difference?

You could return to the other pairs and work with them in subsequent weeks.

---

4) Listen to the stories you tell

So far, we've talked about recognizing the worldly winds, distinguishing between control and influence, and then responding to them in a new way, bringing in some new quality that changes our relationship to them. Now we're going to look a bit more closely at what is happening when we're caught by the worldly winds. We're going to look at the 'stories' that go on in our minds.

When the Buddha gave this teaching of the worldly winds he made it quite clear that they would blow around everyone. But it was the 'spiritually immature' that would be most buffeted by them, he said. Their minds would remain consumed by gain or loss, praise or blame, and so on. Whilst they would welcome the wind blowing one way, they would rebel against it when it blew the other. But a 'well-trained disciple of the Buddha', the text goes on to say, does not become consumed by them, does not 'welcome' or 'rebel'.[27]

Often what this welcoming and rebelling consists of is a story. Much of the time we are telling ourselves a story; we have an ongoing commentary in our head. As we go through our day, we explain and interpret it to ourselves, often only subconsciously.

Stronger emotions give rise to, in a way *are*, the strongest, keenest felt, most urgent stories. For example, someone makes a remark that I find really irritating. Later that day I may notice how I'm playing and replaying that conversation in my head. I tell the story to myself about twenty times, each time embellishing it with more commentary and analysis about how utterly unreasonable they were. I think of clever, scathing remarks that I wish I'd thought of at the time. I fantasize about the final, irrefutable put-down I'll deliver when we meet tomorrow.

These stories can be so quickly triggered. Someone annoys us, and almost immediately there is a fully-formed story in our heads about why they did this, and how they dared do that. How are we able to form quite involved stories so quickly? We draw on our past. The stories are based on the ways we've interpreted our experience on previous occasions. If we've had difficulty with that person before, or even with someone who reminds us of that person, then associations and explanations from our past come readily to mind. Sometimes it is not just our personal past experience that we draw on, but the stories and associations prevalent in our culture. There are 'collective stories' that we all too readily bring to mind. They seem to fit the case and so they 'are' the story of what has happened.

Not only do our interpretations and stories of the past condition the interpretations and stories in the present situation; these then become the interpretations that are readily available in the future. This is one way karma works. We have conditioned ourselves into telling certain stories, and these have a profound effect on the way we experience the world, and how we then respond to it. In a way, we *are* the stories we tell ourselves about our place in the world.

There are stories that are triggered by fear, or ill-will, and there are also stories triggered by longing and craving. Falling in love involves telling ourselves a story, just as falling into hatred and ill-will does. We fantasize, we play and replay situations in our mind. We wonder how he or she will respond if we do one thing, or if we say the other. Often, however, it can be harder to spot the stories that arise out of craving than those that arise out of aversion. The latter are more obviously painful; we can see that the story is only going to end in tears. But stories that arise out of craving can seem more enjoyable and stimulating, a harmless little fantasy. It is easier to believe in them, to convince ourselves that it could end happily ever after.

This tendency to mental commentary and storytelling is referred to by the Buddha as *papañca*,[28] a Pali term which means something like 'mental proliferation', and which describes well the quality and tone of those kinds of thoughts. They do proliferate, breed and spread out all over the place. Sometimes the story seems clear and vivid in our minds; sometimes it is more vague and shadowy. Either way, we create an interpretation of events which may be highly subjective, even quite untrue. We then act unwisely and blunderingly, basing our actions on our own fantasy, our hopes or fears, and not on what is really going on.

How do we work with all this? Once you've noticed what you are doing, slam the brakes on *papañca*. Just try to stop telling those stories. But don't block off from what is happening; stay with the experience underlying the stories. Try to remember what actually happened and to acknowledge your feelings. Stay with the objective situation rather than the subjective interpretation, the bare facts rather than the embellishments.

In other words, separate out observation from interpretation. This doesn't mean not evaluating or judging a situation. If, for example, you've found someone irritating, you may need to think about what their motive was, and so on. You have to make judgements and decisions. But try to make them based on observation, and not on the stories of craving and aversion that are spinning their own interpretations in your head. This is what being judgemental in the negative sense is: an evaluation based on our own longing and fearing. Depending on whether what someone did accords with our own desires, we invent a story about them being a 'good' or 'bad' person.

So, I'm driving along and a man in another car pushes out in front of me. I can immediately start telling myself he is a 'young hooligan who shouldn't be allowed on the roads'. But I don't know. Maybe he is trying to get to a hospital quickly because his child has been taken ill. Maybe he is just like me: a commuter, prone to anxiety and absent-mindedness, who doesn't want to be late for work. Or maybe he is young, pushy and aggressive, but even so, is the label 'hooligan' accurate?

Stopping *papañca* is not easy. Whilst you can sometimes see what you are doing and come to a sharp stop, at other times the stories have a momentum of their own, they press in on you, they sweep you along. The emotions that are driving them are simply too powerful. We go with them because it seems less painful, or more pleasurable. We don't want to face the pain or disappointment of what has actually happened. In these cases, even if we can't stop ourselves straight away, we can still watch ourselves, observe what we're doing, and this will have the effect of gradually helping us to see that the stories are just stories. We just need to keep asking ourselves, gently but firmly, if those stories are really true and helpful.

Of course we cannot avoid all storytelling and commentary. We do need to reflect on our experience and talk with ourselves about it. This is how we learn and become more self-aware. There can be helpful and liberating stories too. The need is to distinguish stories driven by craving and aversion from stories informed by awareness and loving-kindness. Some stories resist and resent the reality of a situation. Other stories face up to what happened and try to imagine a more creative response. We can idly daydream, or we can dare to dream.

For example, there is someone with whom I've had a difficult and painful relationship. I may have a story about how awful and unreasonable he is, and how nothing I do or say will make any difference to his behaviour. A more helpful inner dialogue would consider how I could be different towards him, and would remember that he can change too. It wouldn't be naive or gullible, but would try to imagine a better possibility.

You could say one kind of story arises out of fantasy or 'selfish imagination'; the other kind of story arises out of faith and the 'creative imagination'. You could also call one way of functioning the 'wheel' (going round and round, repeating the same old stories and painful patterns), whilst the other mode is the 'spiral' (rising up into a bigger perspective and experience of the world). The former is reactive; the latter is responsive. We're trying to move from fantasy to faith: not blaming the world for our experience, but responding with confidence that we can grow, learn and develop from it.

Many of the stories we tell are trivial, small-minded. But some stories that take hold in the world have horrific results. It was, for instance, a story that led to the Holocaust. The caste system in India is essentially a story about people and their God-given roles in society. For as long as enough people believe the story, the oppression and deprivation will continue. The underlying process of storytelling is the same, but in this case the outcome is particularly extreme. Stories are powerful transmitters of culture, beliefs and attitudes. (We'll be focusing on two of the stories of our modern Western culture in chapter 5 of the book.)

Reflection: the stories we tell

With kindly awareness, begin to investigate your thought-processes more deeply, to listen to the running commentaries you make, to be more aware of the kind of stories you tell. You are trying to watch the thoughts

*without telling yourself you are a good or bad person for having them –
to do that is just another story you are telling yourself. Just be kind and
understanding towards yourself. Here are three suggestions for how to
go about investigating those stories:*

- *Simply observe your thought processes the next time you notice
  yourself being blown about by the worldly winds. When you
  experience blame, pain, gain, or whatever, do you notice mental
  proliferation kicking into gear?*
- *Or make a practice of watching thoughts in meditation; once your
  meditation has settled, turn your attention to the quality, energy
  and tone of your thoughts, as well as their content (the actual
  story or commentary).*
- *Or, just walking down a street, as you pass people by, ask yourself
  what happens. Do you, ever so subtly and fleetingly, start to
  comment, compare, label and interpret? ('She's good looking, I
  bet he's loaded, he looks a bit rough, I wouldn't trust her as far as
  I could throw her' and so on.) You may start to notice just how
  strong and all-pervasive this tendency to mental proliferation is.*

*In all these cases, notice the quality and tone of the thoughts, as well
as the content of what you are thinking. What is the difference in tone
between these thoughts and thinking that is more reflective and skilful?
Is there a difference in emotional tone, and in the quality of thought?*

*In all cases, stepping back and observing, bringing awareness to these
tendencies to mental proliferation will have a positive effect. It will help
to slow the process down, and allow time for a more skilful response.*

3

Shelter from the storm – the inner work of meditation

The last chapter looked at how, when the worldly winds blow, we need to see them for what they are, and learn to distinguish control from influence. Then we can find a more creative response, bringing a new quality into play, rather than swinging between opposites. We also become more aware of the stories we tell, stories that arise out of that desire to control. Again, if we can see the stories for what they are, step back from them, we can gain a fresh perspective, and new possibilities can open up.

Of course, this is easier said than done. We can't always just let go of our habitual response, or the running commentary in our mind. It is too deeply ingrained, or we're too strongly invested in it. The stories can have a real momentum and emotional force behind them. Bringing them to a halt is a gradual process. Although we can't always stop straight away, as long as we are aware and making some effort to apply the brakes, we will be gradually slowing down our old responses and making a change of direction a possibility.

This chapter is going to approach that process of letting go of old longings and fears – and all the mental proliferation that goes with them – from a different angle: that of meditation. In a way, the last chapter dealt with the 'outer work' of sailing the worldly winds, and this chapter is concerned with the 'inner work'. We're going to be looking at the underlying *process* of meditation. We will try to get underneath particular meditation techniques or practices and examine what is going on mentally and emotionally, the inner dynamic of meditation. The purpose is to understand better how meditation works, so that we can become more skilled at giving up the old, unhelpful, habitual responses, and allowing new possibilities to emerge. We're exploring how meditation can help develop an inner richness and contentment that helps us rise above difficult situations in the world.

To do this, we're going to make use of a traditional Buddhist formulation known as the seven stages of Enlightenment (*bodhyangas*).[29] This appears frequently in the traditional texts, and seems to have been an important teaching from the early Buddhists' point of view. They are a progressive series of qualities that, if developed, will lead us from where we are now towards a state of wisdom and compassion.

We will be using this teaching to explore the role of meditation in bringing about that transformation. The sequence it describes helps make clear how mental and emotional development takes place in meditation, regardless of what practice we are doing. The stages of Enlightenment reveal the progressive and cumulative refinement of consciousness that is meditation. It doesn't happen by magic, or by wilfully applying a technique. Rather it is a natural unfolding, each factor emerging from the preceding ones.

The seven stages of Enlightenment are as follows (with the traditional Sanskrit terms in brackets).

1) Mindfulness (*smṛti*)
2) Investigating and sorting out mental states (*dharma-vicaya*)

3) Energy (*vīrya*)
4) Joy (*prīti*)
5) Calming (*praśrabdhi*)
6) Concentration (*samādhi*)
7) Equanimity (*upekṣā)*

I'm going to go through them one by one, make a few comments on each, and try to show how each one leads naturally to the next.

1) Mindfulness

When you are aware, or mindful, you are more open to your experience. With practice your mind seems clearer, and less scattered and confused. You can be more conscious of what is going on in the world around you, and more in touch with your inner responses to that, your thoughts and feelings about what is going on. There's also a certain sensitivity associated with awareness. The more mindful you are, the more attuned to the subtlety and nuances of things you can be, whether these things are external, such as the colour of a flower, or the emotional well-being of another person, or something internal, such as your own thought processes. It feels good to be aware. When we are more aware, it just seems 'right'; we feel we are more human, more alive, and more rooted in what life is truly about.

How do we cultivate more mindfulness? Often in meditation we are encouraged to start with awareness of the body, and there is a good reason for this. The body (like the breath) is always there, and it is good to start by being aware of something quite simple in the sense of being immediately present in your experience. You can just sit and experience the body: its sensations, weight, posture and feel. You notice its pleasures and pains, energy and aliveness, tension or tightness. Body awareness helps begin the process of tuning into your direct,

53

current experience, whereas thoughts and emotions can, to start with, be more subtle and elusive. Because there can be such a whirl of thoughts, there is more chance they will catch us out, whisking us away into a reverie about the past or an anxiety about the future. Awareness of the body, however, can help ground us in the present.

In this way, the body tells the truth. Through becoming more aware of your body, you also start to become more aware of the mental and emotional factors at play. The pleasures and pains of the body, its energies and where they flow and where they are blocked, often give you clues to your internal states. For example, I might be anxious or angry, but not aware of it. Sometimes I don't want to admit to myself that So-and-so who spoke rudely to me this morning has quite annoyed me. Or, through pride, I've not wanted to let others notice that I'm anxious about the proposal I made at work today, and so I've even got into denial of that anxiety to myself. But the body will tell the truth. If I sit there in meditation, experiencing my body, I will start to become aware of what is really going on. I feel a tightness round the heart area and then start noticing how I'm telling myself the story of how rude that person was – just playing over that little incident in my mind, again and again. Or, I notice a hard knot in one shoulder and a slight queasiness in the belly, and then I start to realize how mentally tired I am. They are the symptoms that show that something deeper down is not right. On the other hand, it may be that I notice energy and relaxation in the body, and feelings of brightness and ease. It is good to look for these more positive signs too, and not just focus on problems and difficulties. It is important to give attention to the full range of your experience.

Once we begin to be aware, to experience the truth, we can, if necessary, start to change it. Mindfulness is the foundation of the meditative process of transformation.

2) Investigating and sorting out mental states

This might sound a bit technical and clunky, but all it means is becoming more aware of what is going on in your mind and heart, and, as part of that awareness, knowing whether thoughts and emotions are skilful or unskilful, helpful or unhelpful, positive or negative.

One effect of body awareness and practice of mindfulness is to slow your mind down, to create spaces between the succession of thoughts, the storytelling. In those spaces you can begin to see more clearly what is going on. Through being more grounded in your body you are able to experience your mental and emotional states more fully. Maybe you've started to notice the feel, and the effects, of anxiety or anger. You realize you want to move away from those states, since they are unhelpful to you (and also to others).

There is an important principle here. We can only begin to 'investigate and sort out' once we've got in touch with our experience. Otherwise we can start trying to mould and control our experience prematurely, in a way that may actually block us off from it. A more open, broad awareness needs to come first, but then we apply a more investigative, discriminative awareness. We need connection before correction.

This stage is not about beating yourself up for unhelpful thoughts or emotions, or wishing you weren't experiencing them, or trying to pretend you're not, or gritting your teeth and saying that if you were a proper meditator you'd be able to make them go away. You just sit, try to remain aware, and try not to engage with negative thoughts and emotions, but to let go of them. You feel their effect, their quality and emotional tone, and continue to let them go. You look at your own actions and responses in the world, not blaming how you feel on others. You are more able to see the stories you've been telling, and have a critical distance from them. You can begin to drop negative, limiting, unhelpful stories. You just say 'no' to them, gently but firmly. You tell them, 'Sorry, but you're not helping, so I'm giving you up.' On the other hand, you allow and encourage positive thoughts and emotions.

If, during meditation, negative thoughts and emotions begin to take off again, it can help to keep returning to the body. Experiencing the body helps us get underneath things a bit more, down into the emotional truth of what is going on. It takes time. Sometimes meditation feels like being tied to a big elastic band. It's like you're inching forward to somewhere better and then – *boing* – you are sprung back to where you started from. So you start inching forward again. You do have to make, and remake, an effort to change. But every time you do that you are stretching and weakening the old habit, you can get a bit further forward, and, even if you rebound, it is with a little less force.

3) Energy

What happens next, again quite naturally, is that positive energy will expand and grow, as energy previously bound up with negative thoughts and emotions begins to be freed up.

Again, this is a continuation of the previous stage. Your energy is starting to switch over from what is negative and constricted to what is positive and expansive. All the energy that was locked in that tense body, or caught up in endless, circular thoughts, or invested in feeling indignation starts to unlock, release, and flow free. You notice that your body becomes a bit more relaxed and easy, your mind becomes a little more calm and lucid, and your heart is more open and light.

You could view meditation as all about converting negative to positive energy. Our physical, mental, and emotional energies are not separate, but are connected to each other. In meditation we gradually learn about this. The branch of the Buddhist tradition known as Tantra is especially concerned with this 'alchemy of energy'. It sees the whole of reality, the whole of life itself, as energy manifesting in different forms. None of these forms is ever fixed. Energy is always potential; it can always change.

So look for energy in meditation. It can be subtle, especially to start with. It may not be pure, positive energy. Often there are different things going on in meditation at exactly the same time, both positive and negative. We can sometimes tend to be problem-orientated and only see the negative. But again, look at the whole range of your experience, and allow any releases of energy. You can subtly, without forcing, use the breath to help with this. Take your awareness to where in the body there is aliveness and as you breath in, imagine more energy; then, as you breath out, allow it to release and flow more smoothly.

4) Joy

'Energy is Eternal Delight', said William Blake.[30] Freed and flowing energy is naturally pleasurable. So the next stage in this unfolding sequence is joy. Meditation should be en*joy*able! Although it may not be so every time we sit, at least sometimes there should be relaxation, letting go, and associated with that, joy. Since it is a pleasure that has arisen out of skilful mental states, you can just enjoy it.

Joy can manifest in different ways and at varying levels. You might experience your body feeling warm, or tears flowing. Or there may be a sense of energy flowing round the body, or even rushing up the spine. You may notice your posture straightening itself, but without your consciously deciding to move. Sometimes there is the sensation of the body filling and expanding with light. Experiences like these are most probably this kind of joy. At other times we do not notice such obvious or dramatic signs of flowing energy. But it may still be the case that energy is being released and, as a consequence, there is a quiet, growing sense of well-being and happiness, a simple sense of gladness and ease.

Again, you can encourage this process by working with the breath. As you breathe in you might say 'joy' quietly to yourself, allowing energy and joy to arise or expand, and then, as you breathe out, you let it flow more smoothly.

All these symptoms of freed energy are a good sign, but they are not the aim of meditation. They are just experiences that, though pleasurable, won't last. In a sense, it is what we do next, what we do *with* this energy and joy, that counts. Sometimes we need to watch ourselves at this juncture, to stay aware and maintain that solid foundation of mindfulness. Maybe you have had meditations that seem to go well, and then all of a sudden you are engrossed in thoughts and fantasies with more gusto than ever before. What happened? Perhaps, although you managed to liberate energy, old habits then kicked back in, taking all that lovely freed energy down old, too-familiar ruts and patterns of thought.

Alternatively, you can have a meditation that brings calm and concentration and think, 'Hey! That was good. I've got this meditation thing sorted now.' You eagerly await your next meditation, when you hope that the same thing will happen again. But when you next meditate, you seem to be beset more strongly than ever before by mental proliferation. What has happened this time? As we have seen, meditation brings about integration; it brings thoughts and emotions more fully into consciousness. Going deeper in meditation allows this to happen more fully; it allows the depths to emerge. So, sometimes when we have a 'good' meditation, we will find that next time there is emotional energy, and accompanying mental activity, that has seemed to come from nowhere. So, in a way, our meditation can seem harder. However, we are now meditating with more of ourselves and this is, of course, a good thing. It will allow even more energy and joy to be freed up.

5) Calming

The next stage is, through remaining aware, to contain and calm the energy and joy. You try to keep it flowing in a positive direction, rather than allowing it to dissipate in the mind's usual thousands of thoughts and concerns. You stay aware of the feelings of physical pleasure and emotional joy, but then, subtly and carefully, shift your focus to the sense of inner happiness and calm that arises naturally from them. You look for contentment, peace, even bliss.

This stage is pivotal in that it represents the 'transition from the psycho-somatic to the mental-spiritual level of experience.'[31] Our meditation is now becoming markedly more concentrated and refined. It is not that we've managed to 'switch off' – as people sometimes say they'd like to do through meditation. It is more that we've unblocked negative energy, then expanded positive energy, but we have done this whilst staying grounded and contained. Peace is a fire; it is not calm in the sense of being damped-down or insipid.

An image suggested by Sangharakshita[32] for this peace is that of a bumblebee hovering around flowers in a summer garden. It stumbles about buzzing loudly and eventually lands on a flower and crawls right in, still humming and droning. But then it finds the nectar, the buzzing stops, and there is a sudden quiet. If we can go within in meditation, we can find the happiness we want, and the buzzing of our mind subsides into silence.

This tranquillity can be experienced through taking part in the Sevenfold Pūjā, a Buddhist ritual involving reciting inspirational verses, chanting mantras, listening to readings, and making offerings of flowers, candles and incense. It is very rich and beautiful, intended to refine and satisfy all our senses, as well as our hearts and minds. Towards the end there is more chanting of mantras and then we chant *śānti*. This means 'peace' and it is chanted three times to signify the peace that comes from the end of all craving, hatred and ignorance. The last *śānti* dies away and we just sit in silence. But it can be such a powerful, full silence. All the inspiration of the pūjā is held still, for a while, in that final hush.

In your meditation, this calm and peace can be cultivated and nurtured out of the preceding qualities of energy and joy. It is difficult to put these subtle, inner experiences into words, so if you don't relate to the following description, don't worry. It doesn't necessarily mean you are doing it wrong! But it is as if the process so far has been more about the physical and emotional release of energy, and there is a kind of upward and outwardly releasing movement to this. This next stage is about that energy stilling and settling; this can feel like a movement downward and inwardly deepening. Again, you can work with the breath, very subtly now, breathing in energy and joy, breathing out and down into a sense of calm, relief, stilling, inner happiness and contentment. You could even say these words very quietly to yourself as an aid.

6) Concentration

What you may find when you sit in the silence at the end of a pūjā, or a period of chanting, is that you want to meditate. You feel naturally still and concentrated. This is because all your energies are flowing, but they are also contained, and you feel happy and content. The mind does not need to cast anxiously around looking for entertainment or occupation. It is already satisfied. True concentration does not come from fixing and forcing the mind on an object such as the breath. It comes from the mind being happy and content, so that it is naturally still and absorbed in the breath.

The mind flaps around much of the time, 'like a fish on hot sand,' as the Buddha once graphically put it.[33] So much of the time the mind reels around, dreaming and designing what it thinks will make us feel secure or important. We may think we are anxious and busy because of the objective demands of the world. But when we meditate we start to see how much of the fuss and worry is subjective. It is we who are driving it!

Sometimes, particularly in meditation, we manage to give up this constant craving and simply be. The Buddhist tradition is telling us that this state of deeper satisfaction is our birthright; this is how we should naturally live. But the person who prevents us receiving our inheritance is our very own self.

At this stage in the meditation, you try to refine your concentration – perhaps by focusing on the breath in just one part of the body. You try not to allow thoughts and distractions to creep back in, but wish instead to enjoy the peace and bliss of absorption.

7) Equanimity

Once the mind is concentrated in this way, it is also more clear and lucid. This creates the foundation out of which equanimity can arise. When your mind is still and concentrated, then it becomes more unshakeable. You see through emotions and thoughts that might normally upset you. You are rooted in a deeper contentment, in an equanimity that can hold firm amidst the ups and downs of life. You are no longer blown by the worldly winds. There is such a deep happiness that you are unconcerned by your usual worries or fantasies; you have a bigger, deeper perspective on them now.

When a spiritual emotion is described in the Buddhist tradition, it is often accompanied by an account of the 'far' and the 'near' enemies of that emotion. By 'far enemy' is meant its complete opposite, the emotional response that lies at the other end of the spectrum. In the case of equanimity, the far enemy is a restless excitement about what is pleasurable or welcome, and a restless anxiety about what is painful or unwelcome.

The 'near enemy' is an emotional response that might seem similar to the spiritual emotion that is being described, and could therefore be mistaken for it. The near enemy of equanimity is indifference. As described by Ayya Khema:

> Indifference is often a protection against emotion. People who have had unhappy experiences, who have been hurt, whose feelings have run away with them, often try to protect themselves from their own negative emotions. But in attempting never to be upset, angry, or full of hate, they actually push down all other emotions too. The result is indifference. Having built a wall around themselves, they no longer have access to their feelings of loving-kindness or compassion.[34]

Indifference can also come out of anxiety or lack of confidence. Not wanting that to be seen by others, we avoid anything that is too difficult, anything that might ruffle our composure, and we pretend that we're not really bothered by it. We tell ourselves that we're above getting rocked about by emotion, but actually all we are doing is keeping the emotion at a safe distance. This can become a whole attitude to life, keeping everything cool and calm, in a way which hardens into indifference. If you are experiencing true equanimity, you do not just look on; you are engaged and passionate, but without being personally, selfishly invested in a particular outcome.

Another near enemy of equanimity can be experienced in meditation. Sometimes, when my meditation has got a bit too wilful, I find myself in a state where there is very little distraction and the mind seems quite still. But then I realize it is not a very pleasant state. It feels inert and lifeless, like a boat becalmed at sea. Or, to extend the metaphor, it is like a ship stranded in a desert – since it is strangely 'dry' and artificial. There is very little feeling or emotion. What has happened is that I have attempted to take a shortcut to concentration and equanimity, without allowing the preceding stages to unfold. Instead there is a wilful holding down of the mind, a concentration of the mind that is devoid of energy and joy – not at all the real thing.

— —

Here is one more image or metaphor for the sequence of the stages of Enlightenment and where they can take us. Imagine you are on board a hot-air balloon that is just taking off. At first it seems rather cumbersome and heavy. Slowly and awkwardly it heaves itself up into the air. There is ballast – unnecessary weight – that you throw overboard, which allows the balloon to rise higher. Then there is a burner that fires up and takes the balloon into a sudden upward rush. You are now pretty high up and can see fields and farms and lanes laid out below. It is all rather exciting. But then the roar of the burner subsides and there is pure, clear silence. The excitement quietens, and is replaced by a sense of awe and a much deeper happiness. All around you is vast blue sky and a sense of space and stillness. You look down on that little world below from a completely different perspective.

What is the practical use of this teaching? Knowing something about the sequence may help us understand what is going on in our meditation. We could start looking for the qualities it describes when we meditate. Often we can be problem-orientated and look for what *isn't* working, or what *isn't* happening. That can be helpful and necessary. But make sure you also look for – and acknowledge – the positive qualities that are likely to be there: the subtle currents of energy, joy, and so on that will be eddying and flowing alongside the rest of your experience.

Maybe you will recognize some of the stages of Enlightenment, or at least elements of them, in your own meditation experience. Some of them may be more present in your meditation than you think. The process of meditation is subtle and some of the words that are traditionally used to describe it may not always seem to match our experience. Words like 'bliss', 'concentration', 'equanimity' can sound like they only refer to big, dramatic experiences, so we can be led into thinking that we never experience all that deep, meditative stuff. Often, however, we underestimate what is happening in our meditation. Even amidst distraction, there can be other currents of energy trickling away. We can learn to work with them, allowing them to flow more fully and deeply.

The effect of meditation will spill out into the rest of your life, though you may not even notice it straight away, or may not make an explicit connection between your meditation and how your life seems to be changing. Again, we can tend to underestimate the effects of our practice. Meditation can give us the inner resources to work with the worldly winds. It is like taking a daily trip in that balloon, rising above the gusts and squalls of the world, and reminding ourselves of the bigger perspective. We come back to the world refreshed and inspired, and more able to deal with the worldly winds again.

Reflection: meditating with the stages of Enlightenment

Meditation is subtle, and quite how it works will vary from person to person. Words and sentences in a book may be able to communicate the general principles, but for the nuances and subtleties it is good to talk to someone else who has an established meditation practice. With that caveat in mind, here are a few suggestions for exploring the teaching of the 'stages of Enlightenment' in your meditation:

- *Use body awareness to ground yourself, and contact what is happening right now.*

- *Look for positive qualities and also watch out for when you are being too problem-orientated. We've covered a lot of positive qualities in this chapter. You could re-read a section or two of the chapter each day, just before you meditate, and then look in your experience for the qualities described – even if they are just there in germinal form.*
- *Use the breath: breathing into and softening areas of the body where there is tension or a blocked feeling, and as you breathe out having a sense of releasing and letting go.*
- *As you breathe in, breathe into and expand energy and joy; as you breathe out, allow relaxation and flow.*
- *As you breathe in, be aware of energy and joy; as you breathe out, sense that deepening-down into calm and contentment.*

Traditionally, the stages of Enlightenment describe the whole process of Awakening or Enlightenment. In other words, in the traditional context of this teaching, equanimity is a synonym for Enlightenment. However, we've been talking about the stages, applying the underlying principles, and seeing how they lead to equanimity in a more immediate, accessible sense. Early on in the spiritual life any equanimity we cultivate tends to last only for a while; the ways of the world are soon able to unbalance it. But gradually, over time, as our practice becomes stronger, the equanimity becomes more firmly established, more part of the natural inclination of our being. It sinks in, bit by bit. Practice makes perfect. Eventually, equanimity becomes something that is fully integrated, fully part of how we see and understand life. It is an equanimity that is so deeply rooted that it will never be shaken. This is what the Buddhist tradition calls Wisdom or Insight, and it only arises on the basis of all that previous practice. This Wisdom is the subject of the next chapter.

4

The winds of change – deepening our perspective

In this chapter we'll be looking more deeply into the nature of the worldly winds, and seeing how they are the winds of *change*. We can experience this constant change, this lack of solidity and predictability of life, as a kind of groundlessness and uncertainness, which we try to deny, or distract ourselves from. The Buddhist spiritual life, on the other hand, is about facing up to change. If we can understand it more deeply, it ceases to be threatening, but becomes full of possibility.

Buddhism says that change is inevitable and unavoidable; the winds of change are always blowing. The way the universe works – what the universe *is* – is a vast, constant, interconnected process of change. The Buddhist tradition uses the term *pratītya-samutpāda* ('conditioned co-production') to describe the way everything consists of changing conditions. Any object, person or situation we come across is made up of a temporary constellation of causes and conditions. These conditions will soon change, and that means the object, person or situation changing.

Because, one afternoon in the 1950s, a West London landlady held a tea party, the man who was her lodger met a young woman and they fell in love. They got married and had children – they were my mum and dad. I had a particular upbringing, with parents with particular histories and temperaments. I grew up in a particular locality in London, which meant I went to particular schools and was taught by particular teachers and made particular friends. There were all sorts of factors specific to the place, the culture, and the times that conditioned who I am. One such factor was that I grew up when Buddhist teachers were beginning to establish sanghas (Buddhist communities) in the West. As a young man I became a Buddhist, and eventually, many years later, came to be writing a book on Buddhism and the worldly winds.

So this book depends on many conditions. Without them, you would not be sitting reading it. No Sangharakshita (the man who founded the Buddhist movement I joined), no book. No landlady holding a tea party, no book. If you trace the conditions further back and further out, you see that they are infinite; there are the conditions that led to my mum and dad's parents meeting, and their parents, and so on.

This might sound obvious or self-evident, especially if we're familiar with Buddhist teaching and we've heard it many times before. However, although on one level we know that we and everything around us are made up of changing conditions, on another level we have an almost instinctual tendency to see things as more separate and fixed. We notice an object, person or situation, and that process of perception, of identifying and recognizing, leads us into seeing them as separate, existing in isolation from all the other conditions around them. Having that sense of them being separate and unaffected by other conditions leads us into seeing things as more fixed and permanent than they really are. It is not that our perception is completely wrong, but it is relatively partial, the result of not looking more deeply into what is going on. Instead of seeing something ephemeral and contingent on all sorts of contexts and circumstances, some brief constellation of possibility, our perception tends to turn it into something much more solid and substantial.

Buddhism isn't interested in all this so we can have clever philosophical discussions about it. It is concerned with these issues because it says they are the root of our suffering, frustration, and lack of fulfilment in life. Buddhism says that because we don't see what is really there, we relate to things in a mistaken way; we have unrealistic expectations of them or make unwarranted assumptions about them. We form views and stories about ourselves and other people, based on our partial perceptions. Often we're doing this quite subtly and unconsciously. We might find someone difficult, and our story about them becomes almost entirely fixated around that difficulty, so that we fail to see them as a more complex, changing, conditioned being. We may have a view of ourselves which is similarly limiting: 'I'm good at this, but useless at that. I like those kinds of things, and I only get on with these kinds of people.' It's as though our minds take snapshots of reality, but then we mistake those small, two-dimensional pictures for the real thing.

We get to know someone and we form an image, or idea, about them. There is nothing wrong with this as far as it goes. But sometimes we start seeing the image – the label – instead of the person. The person may change, but our image doesn't keep up with the change. We see them in the same old way, because we are not actually seeing them, but the outdated image, or the inappropriate label. Our idea of someone, or of ourselves, hardens into a set of assumptions and fixed ideas. Again, this can be very subtle, and we may not be aware we're doing it.

If we relate to changing conditions as solid, enduring entities that we can grasp or repel, we are setting ourselves up for disappointment. Buddhism says that existence in this conditioned universe is bound to involve a degree of unsatisfactoriness. This is not pessimism, but realism. It is not saying there is *only* dissatisfaction, but that it is an unavoidable aspect of life. This is because, in a conditioned universe, we can't possibly expect things always to turn out how we want. But if we get fixed on things turning out a certain way, allowing craving to take hold of us when they work out as we wish, or letting aversion arise when they don't, we create even more frustration. Our denial of reality, our rebelling against it, adds more suffering. In a way, it is like the 'two arrows' of chapter 2. There is an unsatisfactory situation we can't avoid – the first arrow. But then we also fire the second arrow of craving/aversion, longing/fearing, or grasping/repelling. In trying to fix the situation, we actually fix and perpetuate our frustration with it.

Buddhist tradition describes three levels of the unsatisfactoriness that is inherent in conditioned existence. Firstly, there is a physical level of suffering – the pain and discomfort that are part of life. In a conditioned world, these things are unavoidable. Where there is birth, there will also be death. Where there is health, there will also be illness. Where there is gain, there will also be loss. You can't have pleasure without pain; if you've got a human body that has the potential to experience pleasure, then you've also got a human body that has the potential to experience pain.

The next level of unsatisfactoriness is more psychological. Even when we manage to arrange life as we want it, there can be anxiety about trying to keep it that way. At one time I was living on my own and also working mainly from home, again on my own. I began to notice how a lot of my mental chatter was all about me and how I could experience more pleasure and avoid pain. What shall I have for lunch? Shall I nip to the shops and buy some nice food? But then I won't have time to read the paper. Because I was living on my own, I could see a bit more clearly how my mind chuntered on all day about me, me, me. I saw how self-obsessed this could become, constant plotting and planning, laced with low-level anxiety, in order to maximise pleasure and minimise pain. And it was an endless process; as soon as I'd had one experience of pleasure, or even while I was still in the midst of it, I was wondering and worrying about where the next one would come from.

The third level of unsatisfactoriness is more existential or spiritual. On some level we know that this constant craving is unfulfilling, even painful. It can seem unreal, in the sense of being superficial and rather empty. We feel the futility of our situation and we want a different way of being. We sense the hopelessness of our attempts to get the ever-changing world to accord with our desires.

But if conditioned existence is so unsatisfactory, why haven't human beings seen through their delusion and gained Enlightenment long ago? The trouble is that – for a while at least – our attempts to fix and control the universe can work. Human beings are so adaptable, ingenious, scheming and inventive. We come up with so many ways of distracting ourselves from that sense of emptiness. We manage to find temporary relief, just enough to perpetuate the hope of happiness and keep us believing that we may just possibly manage to arrange our world so that it fits in with our desires. So we keep going, keep trying, eventually our strategies become habits, and we become stuck in them, feeling there is no alternative, seeing no way out.

Two tramps wait by a roadside. The landscape is flat, featureless, apart from one bare tree. They are waiting for a character called 'Godot', and when he turns up they will be 'saved' – though the two men are rather vague and unsure as to how, or why. But it seems Godot is their only hope, and so they wait, and try to fill in the time.

This, of course, is the scenario of Samuel Beckett's famous play, *Waiting for Godot*. We watch the two tramps banter and bicker, play word games, discuss religion. Sometimes they argue and decide to part. Then they realize how much they need each other and come back together in a show of affection. They reminisce about the past, wonder about the future. They suddenly panic and worry about whether they are waiting in the right place, or at the right time. Sometimes they can't think of anything to talk about, and there is a long, awkward silence. In that silence you hear the depth of their anguish. When, at last, one of them thinks of something to say, and the conversation kicks off again, you feel their relief. They've avoided the feeling of emptiness – at least for a while longer.

At the end of a long day, a small boy comes along and tells them that Mr Godot says he can't come today, but that he will surely come tomorrow. And so they have to wait again the next day, and, whilst waiting, they try to pass the time . . .

Beckett's play presents this existential dilemma, this terror of emptiness, in a very stark, pared-down way. There are just two men in a barren landscape, desperately trying to fill the time. Our world is much more full, colourful, sophisticated, busy and multi-faceted. But in chapter 5 I'll be arguing that much of it – especially the whole culture of consumerism – is driven by the same sense of existential angst, the same fear of emptiness. We take on important projects, buy the latest products, travel to new and interesting places, or distract ourselves with new technologies. As Estragon, one of the characters in *Waiting for Godot*, puts it, 'We always find something . . . to give ourselves the impression we exist . . .'[35]

But it doesn't have to be like this. We are not stuck in this situation like characters in a Beckett play. Whilst Beckett depicted brilliantly that sense of intense unsatisfactoriness, his plays do not indicate any way out. Buddhism, however, says there *is* another possibility.

Human beings are creatures with a double nature. We have developed a consciousness that can be self-aware. In other words, we can be aware of being aware, aware of 'me' doing something, thinking or feeling, looking or listening, and so on. We're not like animals simply in an experience; our consciousness also knows we are having the experience. This means we can reflect and wonder about that experience, we can think about how it might change if we acted differently. The human mind with that self-awareness can go either of two ways. One way is to try to control and manipulate the world, driven by craving and aversion, struggling to arrange the world to suit our desires. The other way is to turn that ability to reflect, that self-consciousness, back onto the mind itself. We can watch closely how the mind works, and try to see the impermanent, conditioned nature of our experience. Once we face the sense of emptiness, then another possibility opens up.

Enlightened beings are people who have seen, *really* seen, the changing nature of things, and the myriad connections between them – how they affect and condition each other, how they depend on each other. Seeing this, really knowing it, they naturally act in accord, in harmony, with the universe. They don't have unrealistic expectations of life in a conditioned and ephemeral universe. They don't set themselves up for frustration or disappointment in that way. Why would they? They've seen it all so clearly that they will never again become entangled in craving and aversion. They relate to the world out of wisdom, and this also means out of love and compassion – a real appreciation of how suffering arises because of our deluded hope of permanence and perfection.

The worldly winds are the shifting conditions of life against which we can struggle, frantically attempting to control things, deny what is going on, or distract ourselves, or to which we can respond with awareness and understanding. The Buddha sometimes talked about three 'obsessions'[36] – essentially three ways in which our mind gets preoccupied trying to cover over the uncertainty and insecurity of life. The first obsession is craving ('I want, that's mine'), the second is conceit (comparing ourselves to others to see if we're better than, worse than, or equal to them), and the third is ignorance (the basic underlying delusion that we can 'fix' reality). When we're blown around by the worldly winds of pleasure and pain, or gain and loss, we're in the grip of craving. We think that we can fill the gap, the sense of emptiness, by grasping hold of some pleasant experience or possession. When fame and infamy, or praise and blame, are blowing us about, then conceit has dominated our mind. We want attention and approval to make us feel solid and real. All these situations are underpinned by that basic ignorance, or unawareness, of reality.

The spiritual life is a battle between the side of us that doesn't want to look at these things, wants to blunder on in unawareness, and the side of us that senses the futility of this, and (like Gautama remembering the rose-apple tree) is beginning to intuit another possibility.

The 'Dharma-doors' of chapter 2 were an opening into that possibility. We can turn the worldly winds into spiritual opportunities, seeing them as teachers that show us how we need to understand reality more deeply. We are training ourselves to respond *to* the world, rather than expecting everything we crave to come *from* the world. Rather than oscillating between gain and loss, for example, we decide to practise generosity. Implicit in this is a realization that holding onto things selfishly is deluded, and that giving up on that, and realizing our connection with others, is more real, and ultimately more satisfying.

Unhelpful, ethically unskilful responses to the worldly winds constitute denial or avoidance of the reality of change. Helpful, ethically skilful responses contain an implicit awareness, or understanding, of that reality. There is wisdom inherent in them. In other words, ethics is connected to wisdom. Buddhist ethics are not based on arbitrary rules, or on belief in some supernatural power, but on 'how things are'; they are the ways a human being can choose to act with more awareness and understanding of how the universe works. An action is ethical *because* it accords with how things are. Buddhist ethics are descriptions of what such actions would be like. Ethical guidelines such as the five precepts[37] are an expression of this in general principles, so that by following them, we can learn to act more in accord with reality.

Then we practise meditation. Part of what happens in meditation is that we begin to notice the stories we tell, and see how they are often expressions of our deluded perceptions of things. They, also, are attempts to make ourselves feel real, to try to secure ourselves in an ever-changing, contingent world. In meditation we try to drop those old unhelpful stories and instead carefully observe our actual experience.

As we train ourselves in this way it gradually – over years of practice – sinks in. Gradually there comes a shift and we see reality as it really is. The old perceptual processes still function, but overlaid by a new awareness. This new awareness becomes less of a conscious effort. It is no longer something we have to remind ourselves of constantly, but naturally part of how we function. It is not anything weird or mysterious; it is simply a deeper, wiser understanding of life.

We gradually develop a more even-minded attitude to the world, even amidst storms and unrest. We are not even-minded in the sense of feeling less, or being less passionate. In fact, because our energy is less taken up in anxiety, we are more able to appreciate and enjoy. There is an increased sensitivity and openness to the world. We are less fixed on certain outcomes, more able to be open to different possibilities, more flexible and adaptable. There is even a growing sense of timelessness; for it is our craving and aversion that pile the pressure of time upon us. We still care deeply and passionately about things in the world, and yet at the same time we are not personally invested in the outcomes.

Reflection: Watching the winds of change

Here is an exercise for seeing the impermanence of the worldly winds. You may be able to bring this teaching of impermanence to mind if and when you are rocked by the worldly winds during your day. You might also reflect more closely and deeply on it when sitting quietly, or meditating.

- *See the impermanence of gain, fame, praise and pleasure*
  Be aware of the 'positive' worldly winds in your life and remind yourself that they will not last. It may seem perverse to deliberately remind yourself that things you like will come to an end, but try it and see what happens! It may give you a different perspective on the pleasant experiences in your life – one that is more calm and appreciative.

  This reflection requires a basis of loving-kindness – you are not trying to cultivate indifference, or pessimism, or even cynicism. If this happens, then just leave this reflection; it is not the right time for you to do it.

- *See the impermanence of loss, infamy, blame and pain*
  You can also look at the 'negative' worldly winds in your life and see how they change, how they come and go, and don't always stay the same. Realizing that those negative experiences won't last forever may help you have a lighter attitude to them. It changes your perspective.

- **See the impermanence in both the 'positive' and the 'negative' worldly winds**

  Then bring both these reflections together and consider the impermanence of both those experiences you like and those you dislike. There is a reason for doing this. The first two reflections can become subtly self-referential – the second one especially can evolve into an exercise in finding a way the situation suits me, and make me happy. So this third reflection goes deeper and sees that in every experience there is change and impermanence.

5

Winds from
the West

The worldly winds always blow, but their particular force and direction changes according to the prevailing circumstances. Though the worldly winds blow today just as they blew in the time of the Buddha, their effects are different. In this chapter we'll be looking at some of the ways they howl and whisper through modern culture.

The last 250 years or so have seen huge changes, occurring first in Western societies, and increasingly spreading to other parts of the world. Advances in science revolutionized agriculture and industry. This led to great upheavals in living and working, production and economy (usually involving a change from a feudal to a capitalist society). Increased trade and commerce led, in time, to more travel and communications, more permeable national boundaries, and a more globalized world.

In pre-modern societies life could be 'nasty, brutish and short'. After the turmoil of industrialization came increased living standards and material comfort. People lived longer, healthier lives, and had increased access to education and culture. But there was a dark side. Whilst economic liberals contend that economic freedom creates prosperity for all in the long-term, others will argue that the wealth of the richer nations depends on exploitation of the poorer. The twentieth century was also one of terrible warfare, and now there is the threat of terrorism, and the growing possibility of ecological disaster.

All these changes have had a profound effect on humanity's view of itself, and of its place in the universe. Though the apparent success of science in explaining the universe has not led to the dying out of religious perspectives as some predicted, they have taken a severe battering. Whereas in pre-modern societies there were ethical frameworks – Christian, Muslim, Buddhist, Jewish, Hindu, Confucian, and so on – today there is no longer such widespread acceptance of agreed frameworks, underpinned by a common vision of what human life is about.

That, put very simply in just a few sentences, is our modern 'Western' world. But because we're in it, and it is the only world we know, it is very easy to take it for granted, to assume it's the only possible kind of world, and to forget just how recent a phenomenon it is. In chapter 2 we looked at how we tell stories to ourselves. We have a narrative, an underlying view, a subtext, that runs – more or less consciously – though our minds, explaining the world and our place in it. We do need stories. Some of our stories are helpful and true, allowing us to interact with the world with creativity. But some of them are fictions of our selfish imagination. These stories can be habitual; the stories I tell myself today are conditioned by the stories I've been telling all my life. Likewise, the stories I tell today will condition how I'll tend to interpret and view the world in the future.

There are collective stories too – narratives, underlying views, subtexts that arise in the cultures that we belong to. These are stories that we all tell to some extent and, like our own individual stories, they contain assumptions about our lives and how to find happiness. We may be more or less aware of these stories. Again, the process of storytelling can become habitual; the stories help shape our response to the world, which shapes the world, which shapes the stories that other people tell, which shape the stories we tell ourselves in the future, and so on.

We're going to look at just two of the stories prevalent in wealthy cultures of the twenty-first century. Though they are not the only stories, they are arguably two of the most fundamental and influential ones. They are what I'll call 'scientism' and 'consumerism'. Scientism is an explanation of the universe, and consumerism is a story about how to find happiness in that universe. They arc like modern religions, filling in the gap left by the decline of the old faiths. They are explanations of our role and purpose that orientate and motivate how we act. They are ideological[38] in the sense that they can appear neutral and value-free, but actually they contain a view about human life, its purpose and meaning, and how to find happiness and avoid pain. They are belief-systems that are all around us in society: in the media, in the high street, in workplaces. They may affect us without our realizing it. They are like the air: ever-present, all around us, but invisible, silent. Yet we are breathing them in all the time. They are self-perpetuating; they make it seem as though this world is the only possible world, and hence they reinforce the status quo. Again, because we're in this world and it is the only one we know, its stories are the only ones we encounter. This can make it difficult to see them clearly.

Another way of looking at scientism and consumerism is that they contain a view about how to deal with the worldly winds. They are stories that say we can control the worldly winds through technology and material progress. We can create a perfect world, one in which there is only pleasure, gain, fame and praise. But, as we know, the worldly winds can never be entirely controlled, and so these stories only create and perpetuate an unhelpful myth, an illusion.

In this chapter I am going to argue against the two stories of scientism and consumerism, and their subtexts, their underlying views of what human life is about, their false promise that we can control and manipulate the worldly winds. I am going to suggest that Buddhists have a role to play in our culture, critiquing and struggling against those limiting, partial stories, and promoting a deeper, fuller story of what human life can be about. The word struggle is used deliberately: it *is* a struggle to free ourselves of views that are all around us. The Dharma is not just a private, personal, individual matter; it is also about helping to create a better world, a more enlightened world, one where people have more opportunity to lead lives of depth and meaning. The problems of our world require a spiritual response.

To free ourselves, we need to be aware of our stories about the world. This means being aware of our moment-by-moment individual stories. But we also need to be aware of the collective stories of the culture, and of the conditions that create and perpetuate them.

— ~

Science is a way of observing and understanding the objective world; the knowledge gained allows us to control that world to our own advantage. It gives rise to various technologies. Scien*tism* is not the activity of science itself, but an ideology about science and its role in our lives. Many people have an active interest and involvement in science without subscribing to scientism, though because of the sheer success of science and its ubiquitous role in our world, it is hard not to fall into scientist views.

Scientism is the belief that 'science is, or can be, the complete or only explanation'.[39] Because science is such a great cultural and intellectual achievement, and so successful in explaining the material world and enabling technologies that improve the material quality of life, we are drawn into making a number of conclusions about it that don't really hold. For example, scientism sees an inevitable march of progress. In the view of scientism, anything science does not already know, it will soon discover and explain, in terms similar to those of current science. There is an inbuilt assumption that the explanation will be a materialist one, that everything will one day be explained in terms of the interaction of physical matter. (You can see this in popular science books where the author explains how theoretical physicists will soon come up with a 'theory of everything', or that evolutionary psychologists will soon explain consciousness.) Scientism also believes that any human problem will have a scientific, technical solution. (So, in the last decade, the US Bush government could, apparently in all seriousness, suggest that satellites orbiting the earth, with mirrors to deflect the sun's rays, could be the solution to global warming, or that satellites with missiles to take out enemy nuclear missiles were the solution to the arms race.) In the view of scientism, we can just go on controlling and manipulating the objective world in order to get what we want.

Consumerism is a story arising out of the world made possible by science, technology and the economic system. It is the belief that we can attain happiness from buying and owning material things. It follows that if we have more money, we can buy more things, which will mean more happiness. My needs for security, self-esteem, connectedness and authenticity can be met through consumption. What I buy and own is, in a sense, an extension of me – it reflects who I am, my values, tastes and unique individuality. So, I need things in order to be me, and in order to impress other people, to be taken seriously by them. The purpose of life is to have as much enjoyment as possible, and this can be achieved – it is possible to have total comfort and happiness, a perfect, ideal life.

This overlaps with another story – that our current economic system is necessary and inevitable. When a global financial crisis hits, the politicians tell us we have to consume more in order to ensure economic growth, and we need economic growth in order that we can go on consuming more. Buddhist writer David

Loy describes 'the market' as the first religion to become truly worldwide.[40]

These stories may sound crude and unbelievable when stated so baldly. But they are there in our culture. Have a look, for example, at how the media covers science stories; you may often detect the values of scientism. Look at the proportion of newspapers that is taken up with the values of consumerism – pages and pages of cars, gadgets, food, holidays, clothes, and articles about rich and famous people and their lifestyles.

~ ~

So what is wrong with these stories?

Scientism tends to ignore the dark side of science. In the last few years there have been a number of bestselling books by authors who are aggressively atheist and anti-religion – a phenomenon that has become known as the 'new atheism'. Often these books are driven by a scientist agenda. Whilst very keen to point out the dark side of religion (how organised religion has, undeniably, often been corrupt, promoted harmful superstition, and encouraged hatred and violence towards non-believers) they don't draw attention to the problems to which science has given rise – the threat of nuclear warfare, ecological problems, and so on. This is because scientism is not an objective, neutral story; it is an ideology, a view about human life. It assumes materialistic, non-religious explanations of the world and our place in it.

Scientism tends to see technology as inherently good. Sometimes people kick against this and see it as bad. But, of course, technology (like organised religion) can be either good or bad. It is a human creation, and depends on the human beings who are using it. For example, the internet can put old school friends back in touch, it can publish information to expose repressive regimes and it can make Buddhist teachings available for free, anywhere in the world. The internet can also be a means of endless superficial distraction, a market for peddling pornography and a forum for repressive regimes to push their propaganda.

Technology is not inherently morally good or bad, but it is not neutral either. The format of a technology has an effect, even a subtle ethical effect. In the case of the internet, the format favours bite-sized, fast-changing pieces of information, between which the user can make endless choices, flicking from this to that with a click of the mouse. That has a profound effect on how people absorb information, how they pay attention to things. In short, it changes consciousness. Technologies are also not neutral because of the context out of which they emerge; they 'cannot be separated from the larger social, economic, and ecological contexts within which they are devised and applied'.[41]

Scientism tells us that science will soon explain the universe, but how much has it really told us? As philosopher Bryan Magee explains:

> Physics, for example, reduces the phenomena with which it deals to constant equations concerning energy, light, mass, velocity, temperature, gravity, and the rest. But that is where it leaves us. If we then raise fundamental questions about that ground-floor level of explanation itself, the scientist is at a loss to answer. This is not because of an inadequacy on his part, or on science's. He and it have done all they can. If one says to the physicist: 'Now please tell me what exactly *is* energy? And what are the foundations of this mathematics you are using all the time?' it is no discredit to him that he cannot answer. These questions are not his province. At this point he hands over to the philosopher. Science makes an unsurpassed contribution to our understanding of what it is that we seek an ultimate understanding of, but it cannot itself be that ultimate explanation, because it explains phenomena in terms which it then leaves unexplained.

> To many working scientists, science seems very obviously to suggest an ultimate explanation, namely a materialist one; but a materialist view of total reality is a metaphysics, not a scientific theory. There is no possibility whatsoever of scientifically proving, or disproving, it.[42]

Again, there is a materialistic assumption, which glosses over the fact that we do not know what matter is. To quote the philosopher Wittgenstein: 'We feel that even when all possible scientific questions have been answered, the problems of life remain completely untouched.'[43] Although science can open us up to the mystery and wonder of things, scientism closes it down again. It directs our attention away from how mysterious and unfathomable the universe is.

It is not science that is the problem, but scientism. It is not the discoveries of science, but their interpretation – the ideology of a dead, material world that we can use and manipulate to our own benefit. This is a problem because it puts us into a wrong, unrealistic relationship to the world, and also because it underplays the mystery and wonder of the realms of faith, imagination and consciousness. These views, and an accompanying suspicion of 'religion', are very influential and prevalent in our culture. They encourage a way of life in which people do not explore and experience the most profound regions of the soul. And that is a tragedy. It is not that the lives people lead as a result are necessarily bad, but that they could have so much more depth, profundity and meaning. To quote Bryan Magee again: 'Some such atheistic humanism has been one of the characteristic outlooks of Western man since the Enlightenment, and is particularly common among able and intelligent individuals . . . It lacks all sense of the mystery that surrounds and presses so hard on our lives: more often than not it denies its existence, and in doing so is factually wrong.'[44]

Consumerism is also a mixed blessing. The degree to which it can produce human happiness is limited. Again, sometimes we might kick against it, and swing into the other extreme – a negative, somewhat puritanical attitude to material things. (Sometimes this is what religions do.) But it is not material things in themselves that are the problem; it is our relationship to them, our hopes and expectations of what they can give us. Some of what is on offer in our society is genuinely life-enhancing: medical treatment to improve the quality of life, access to the world's finest music, and so on. But the story consumerism tells us is that we can rely *totally* on material goods to provide happiness and avoid pain.

The culture of consumerism has recently been gaining attention from researchers in psychology, sociology and economics. The research has discovered that the extent to which consumerism can produce happiness is limited. For example, since the Second World War there have been surveys asking people in North America to rate their happiness. Apparently, happiness ratings peaked in 1957. Since then, people have got no happier, if anything slightly less happy. However, income and consumption levels have more than doubled since 1957. Surveys also ask people what income they'd need in order to be happy. In less than ten years, between 1986 and 1994, their estimate had more than doubled.[45] In America, real income per head (allowing for inflation) has nearly doubled since 1972, yet the proportion of people satisfied with their financial situation has fallen.[46] There is a similar picture in many developed countries: we have more, we think we need even more still, and yet we are no happier.

Why should this be so? I'm going to make use of the schema of the worldly winds to explore this question. Scientism and consumerism can be seen as stories about how to deal with the worldly winds. They are our stories about how technology and material wealth can give us control. But this is a delusion, a collective spiritual unawareness. Gain and loss, pleasure and pain, and so on, are just facts of life. Although they have various effects, according to the prevailing conditions, they cannot (as we saw in the last chapter) be avoided in a conditioned world. We may try to build a 'Western' heaven-haven where the worldly winds don't blow. But they will just blow in new ways: 'westerly' worldly winds.

Firstly, there blow the worldly winds of gain and loss. Through consumerism we may gain material possessions, but there is a corresponding loss in the time taken to earn money to buy them, and in looking after, maintaining and cleaning our homes, cars, and possessions. We're always in a hurry. The car needs servicing. The kids are going abroad on a school tip and need taking to the doctor's for their vaccinations. The guinea pig food has run out. Whilst in some countries working hours have fallen, in the UK and USA they have risen.[47] This has a knock-on effect on the quality of our relationships, family lives and communities. We arrive home exhausted and all we feel able to do is zone out in front of the TV. New technology like e-mail and mobile phones is supposed to make our working lives easier, but the effect is that we take our work with us wherever we go. Last year I was out hill-walking with a friend and, just as we got to the top of a mountain, he got a call from the office. And, because he is a conscientious fellow, he answered it.

We also quickly get used to material gain – what the researchers call 'hedonic adaptation'. The pleasure of material possessions – a new car, an exotic holiday, a meal at an expensive restaurant – soon wears off. More qualitative pleasures last longer – meaningful work, or a deeply felt human relationship.[48]

Then blow the winds of praise and blame. I was once in a queue in a shop a couple of weeks before Christmas, and I got talking to the woman in front of me. It turned out she was feeling quite stressed and harassed by everything she felt she had to do to prepare for Christmas, and to provide for her family and friends. She said she knew it was crazy, how much we are expected to buy, prepare and provide, but she felt she couldn't stop. And the strange thing was that other people in the queue were listening in and nodding in agreement. It was one of those little moments where a façade dropped away and you saw what was going on behind it. The woman really was quite tired and tense because of expectations about what a 'good mother' would provide at Christmas. Whether the expectations came from her family, or just from herself, isn't the point. The fact was that she felt a sense of expectation and that she had to obey it, even if it wasn't what she wanted for herself, or felt to be right. It was a modern consumerist experience of being blown around by the winds of praise and blame.

Many parents know this feeling well. They see the peer pressure their children are under. Then their son Johnny pleads with them to buy them a new gadget. They know that the parents of Johnny's best friend have bought one for their son, and they wonder what they should do. Apparently the marketing people are well aware of this phenomenon – it is known as 'pester-power'!

Research has revealed that one reason why having more often doesn't make us happier is that our happiness is largely based upon comparisons we make with others around us. One piece of research looked at the happiness of people in East Germany before and after unification. Although people became wealthier after unification, their self-rating of happiness fell. What was going on? The researchers concluded that the groups to which East Germans were comparing themselves had changed. Before unification, they contrasted themselves against people in other Soviet-bloc countries. Since they were doing relatively well, they felt happy. After unification, they began measuring themselves with West Germans. They weren't doing as well as them, and so they felt less happy – despite their increased income.[49]

Certain goods become 'necessities' and we cannot imagine living without them. How does this happen? Again, it is about comparison. When other people around us start owning them, they become the signs of a sophisticated, comfortable life. They become the new yardstick by which we measure how well we are doing. In 1970, 20% of Americans thought a second car was a 'necessity'. In 2000, 59% of them thought so. 22% of them saw home air conditioning as 'necessary' in 1970. Thirty years later it was 70%.[50] Twenty years ago, most people had a phone in their house. Now most people expect to have two or three phones dotted round the house, and a mobile phone. Personal computers have been around for only about twenty-something years, the internet for half that time. But it is easy to forget what a fast-changing world we live in; we quickly adapt, we get used to it, we take it for granted. In fact, we come to feel that it is normal for us always to have more, for living standards to go on rising.

Then there is the way the worldly winds of pleasure and pain blow through the culture of consumerism. At every turn we are provided with opportunities for amusement and distraction, ways of trying to find some pleasure to take away our boredom or pain. You see it on commuter trains at the end of a long, hard day. Watch that tired-looking man flicking through the free newspaper. His eyes are skating over the surface of the page, but he is hardly taking anything in. He keeps turning over the pages in the hope of finding something to take his mind off the dull journey and the feeling of tiredness. But it is not working. It is shallow and unsatisfying, and it just returns him to himself even more tired and dull.

Consumerism promises comfort. It is a story that says that we're the customer and we should expect better service. We should demand convenience. However, Buddhist teacher Pema Chödrön says that being immersed in comfort is a form of laziness: 'At the first hint of heat, we turn on the air conditioner. At the first threat of cold, we turn up the heat. In this way we lose touch with the texture of life.'[51] This constant comfort is, in the end, quite dulling and not the same as real happiness. We can become like over-fed animals – placid when full and content, but becoming aggressive if we don't get what we want, or if something inconvenient occurs. If a machine is not working, we get sharp and snappy. If the engineer can't fix it straight away, we virtually howl with rage.

Finally, there are the sharp worldly winds of fame and infamy that blow so fiercely through this culture of consumerism. Again, they've blown throughout history, but in the age of mass communications they have reached gale force. Newspapers, TV channels, internet sites all compete for our attention, so that they earn advertising revenue and make a profit. The more intense the competition, the greater the tendency towards sensationalism, towards stories and pictures that have the most immediate impact, that stimulate our senses and hook our emotions. 'Western society is a permanent emergency:'[52] the voices of the newsreaders become ever more grave and urgent, the headlines more blaring, the pictures more graphic.

Social networking sites, magazines and chat shows are endlessly taken up with the lives of the rich and famous. Their affairs and divorces, their spending sprees and diets, their high-adrenaline lifestyles and drug problems are all given the oxygen of publicity. What is the fascination of fame? There is probably something instinctual about it. We're social creatures; as humans evolved and struggled to survive in a harsh natural world, they did so by living in groups. Those groups would have norms of behaviour, and not to conform would be dangerous. There would also be ways (perhaps being good at tracking wild animals, for example) to gain approval, which would be rewarded with the biggest share of food, or the best mate.

We have an almost primeval urge to fit in, but also to stand out. This instinct has endured through human history. We still want to be different enough to be interesting, but similar enough to fit in. Leo Braudy writes that the urge to fame is an intensification of this desire to be a 'socially-acceptable individualist'.[53] This is what the myth of fame is about: we believe that the famous are liberated from group norms, free to be authentically themselves. Because they are free to be different, they stand out, gain more attention, and that means they are more loved and special. We think the famous are more successful, and therefore wealthier, and thereby even more free and happy.

But it is an illusion, and we can become trapped, oscillating between desire for fame and fear of infamy. To quote David Loy again:

> The irony of a celebrity-obsessed culture is that, whether you're famous or a nobody, you are equally trapped if fame is important to you – that is, if fame is your way to become more real . . . It makes no difference whether I actually am famous. In either case, I'm trapped in the same dualistic way of thinking. If I'm not famous, I will worry about remaining that way. If I am famous, I will also worry about remaining that way – that is, about losing my fame. Although the media needs celebrities they are readily replaced . . . When fame symbolizes becoming more real, disappointment or disillusionment is inevitable. No amount of fame can ever satisfy if it is really something else that I am seeking from it, which it cannot provide.[54]

Fame promises freedom to be oneself, but 'to be talked about is to be part of a story, and to be part of a story is to be at the mercy of storytellers – the media and their audience. The famous person is thus not so much a person as a story about a person . . .'[55] The media are only too pleased to tell us when the famous fall off their pedestals – a politician in a financial scandal, a rock star booking into rehab, or a footballer caught with a prostitute. The contrary worldly winds of fame and infamy shape the simplistic, judgemental way the story is portrayed.

Fame is not necessarily bad. If we're not fooled by its false promises, it may be possible to use it skilfully. We saw in chapter 2 how the Buddha was, in the context of his time and place, 'famous'. People from all walks of life, including kings and military leaders, flocked to see him. But he wasn't taken in by the allure of fame. The Dalai Lama has been cited as a modern example of someone who is recognized the world over and has managed to use that fame to promote non-violence and compassion.

But the deepest, most fundamental reason why consumerism won't produce happiness is that we don't get happiness from material possessions. Happiness is the fulfilment that comes from being meaningfully engaged in our life, from having positive values that we are able to live by, and from quality relationships that express and deepen our care for others. For all these reasons and more, the culture of scientism and consumerism cannot protect us from the worldly winds, despite its promise to do so. The worldly winds still find a way to blow right through.

＿＿＿

How can we respond to these stories about controlling the worldly winds? How can we promote a more human, true and realistic response to them? The remainder of this chapter is going to suggest that a Buddhist life in the modern world requires these four things:[56]

1) Self-development
2) Withdrawing support from institutions, groups and forces in society that perpetuate a limited, materialistic vision

3) Speaking out: critiquing limited ideologies, and communicating real vision and values
4) Joining a spiritual community and helping it to grow

1) Self-development

If we want to be a force for good in the world, we have to start by developing ourselves. We need to nurture the qualities, such as awareness, patience, generosity and kindness, which enable us to engage with the world helpfully. As Sangharakshita expresses it:

> Self-development always comes first. However active you might be in all sorts of external areas – political, social, educational, or whatever – if you are not trying to develop yourself, you are not going to be able to make any contribution to anything or anyone.[57]

2) Withdrawing support from institutions, groups and forces in society that perpetuate a limited, materialistic vision

We can't entirely avoid consuming things, but we can reduce consumption, and we can also try to avoid the values of consumerism as much as possible. One aspect of doing this is to consume as ethically as we can, to buy from companies that are trying to trade fairly, or that put a portion of their profits to socially beneficial use.

We may find ourselves moaning about the huge bonuses bankers are paying themselves, right after the banking sector has caused meltdown in the world economy, and governments have had to bail out the banking system using taxpayers' money. But we can do something, not just moan! There are some small but still significant things we can do. For example, you could change banks and choose the most ethical, responsible bank you can find. Write and tell your old bank why you are leaving them.

At the time of writing, 'bankers' have become villains in sections of the media and society. But of course people who work in the financial sector are human beings. They are driven by the same desires for pleasure, gain, praise and fame as anyone else. It is easy to criticize what appears to be the most extreme and unjust forms of greed, but aren't we ourselves driven by the same forces? We may not be in line for a million-pound bonus, but do we still use money and possessions to prop up a feeling of security, or to attain status? We might ask ourselves questions like: How do I compare myself to others? Does it sometimes motivate what I buy, or how I act? Like the women in the queue at Christmas cited above, do I sometimes feel under pressure to conform?

It is not that we can't criticize specific instances of greed and injustice, but it is no use demonizing one section of society. If we're honest about it, we can see that many of those who complain are doing so because they are caught up in the same game: gain and loss, or praise and blame. We need to critique those underlying values whenever they manifest.

Similarly, it is no use blaming the media for their apparent obsession with fame and infamy. They do it because it hooks us; it is what they think we want. So we could also look at choosing our sources of information ethically – thinking about how much information we need, and what the most truthful, reliable sources are.

Another important way of consuming ethically is to become vegetarian. If you are already vegetarian, then you could consider taking it a stage further and becoming vegan. I notice that people like me who've been vegetarian for years can think, 'I'm already doing the first precept'[58] and settle for that. Maybe, however, this is what Buddhist tradition calls 'rites and rituals as ends in themselves'. We get so used to doing something that it becomes automatic, and we forget the purpose behind it. I sometimes think Buddhists do this with vegetarianism. We've got so used to being vegetarian that we've almost stopped thinking about the non-violent impulse behind it. We forget that dairy products also involve violence to animals. For a cow to produce milk (and hence cheese and cream) she has to have a calf each year, and those calves are then reared for the beef industry.

There is also the fact that a vegan diet has a significantly lower carbon footprint than a vegetarian one, which has a significantly lower footprint than a meat diet. One study estimated that the farming of animals caused more emissions (18% of the total) than the world's entire transport system (13.5%).[59] This has very important implications for the ecosystem and for sustainable development. We eat several times every day, so this is an important area of ethical practice. Do think about whether you could become vegetarian – maybe starting with a few meals per week. Or, if you're already vegetarian, consider becoming vegan – or at least eating a few vegan meals each week.

3) Speaking out: critiquing limited ideologies and communicating real vision and values

Whenever you get the opportunity, speak out and critique the more limited, partial stories of our culture, and try your best to communicate a better possibility. You don't have to become a Buddhist bore, or a ranting preacher; just watch for genuine openings, possibilities for real communication. Just talk about what your experience is. Some people will be interested, even inspired and relieved to discover there are people who are trying to live by different values.

If you have children, talk to them about the nature of consumerism. Be aware that they'll copy what you do and, in large part, learn their values from you, and don't be afraid to use that influence skilfully. If they plead with you to buy something, empathize, but discuss with them why they want it so badly. (This doesn't necessarily mean not buying it; you're just trying to encourage a healthy relationship to material things.) You could play games where you spot the tricks of adverts. Be aware that the TV and internet will be socializing your children into the values of consumerism, but you have an influence too. In the short term they might not thank you for it! But all the research strongly suggests that, in the long term, if they don't get so caught up in the values of consumerism, they will be happier, and they *will* thank you for that.

4) Joining a spiritual community and helping it to grow

What is really needed is a vision of human life, and values that guide and orientate such a life. It is very difficult to uphold that vision and those values on our own, especially amidst all the ups and downs of worldly life. It is much easier (though still challenging!) to do it with the support and friendship of others who share our vision and values. We can probably do more to influence the world (point 2) and to speak out (point 3) by collaborating with others too.

This is why spiritual community is so vitally important. Find a band of like-minded people who you can work with. Do what you can to help the spiritual community to thrive and grow: supporting Buddhist events and classes, helping with publicity, being friendly to new people who turn up, giving financial help, whatever it is. Vibrant spiritual communities are what the world really needs.

This chapter has taken a quick sweep through many complex issues. We focused on two particularly central and fundamental stories of our Western culture, though they are not the only stories. Our culture has much that is positive, and we have a lot to be grateful for, but there are also aspects of that culture that limit and distort human potential. Scientism and consumerism promise an escape from the worldly winds, but it is a false promise. We need to be more aware of their limitations, critique and resist them, and see that the real solution to the blowing of the worldly winds is a spiritual one.

6

If . . .

Kipling's famous poem 'If –' is about what happens if we're able to rise above the trials and tribulations of life, if, for example, we can 'meet with Triumph and Disaster, And treat those two impostors just the same'.[60] But it is not just a question of *if;* it is a matter of *practice.* If we can train ourselves to respond more creatively, if we can reflect on the winds of change, if we can meditate on equanimity, *then* we will change. We will go through life more safely, and be more able to help others do so. This last chapter is going to look more at how such practice works, how – breath by breath – it sinks in and becomes part of us, a natural perspective we have on life, rather than something we have to constantly strive to remember. The last two chapters have been more 'big picture'; this chapter focuses in again, homing in on a few down to earth suggestions for making your practice more effective amidst the busyness of everyday life.

We've gone over a lot of ground fairly quickly in this book – a whole guide to sailing the ocean of the world and its prevailing winds. As we review what we've covered, you'll see that in the course of the book we've gradually gone deeper into the underlying nature of the worldly winds.

1) Become aware of, and name, the worldly winds

The first stage of practice was simply naming the worldly winds, learning to recognize when they are blowing in our lives. It may be that we tend to notice the 'negative' worldly winds (those that we experience as unwelcome and unpleasant) more quickly and easily than the 'positive' ones (those we experience as welcome and pleasant). But it is good to notice both sides of the picture; both can knock our equanimity off course. Just being aware of and naming the worldly winds in this way has an effect. We are creating space around them, stepping back from them, creating the conditions for a more considered response to them.

2) Distinguish control from influence

Part of navigating the worldly winds more skilfully is recognizing where and when you can influence a situation, and where and when you just have to let go and accept the situation you are in. In truth, we can never really control circumstances, but we can usually have some influence on them.

3) See the winds as opportunities, not obstacles

The next step is 'turning them around', seeing the worldly winds as teachers, as opportunities rather than obstacles that are just getting in the way. Changing the metaphor, we look for the 'Dharma-door', the quality through which we change our relationship to the situation.

4) Be aware of the stories you tell

Then, taking our awareness of these situations deeper, we look at the underlying story, or mental commentary, that we tell to ourselves when the worldly winds are blowing. We learn to distinguish stories that are unhelpful products of the 'selfish imagination' (just fantasies about how the world should give us what we want), from the 'creative imagination' (a more aware, considered, creative response to the world).

5) Develop equanimity

If the stories and mental proliferations can be slowed down, we can see them with more clarity, and reflect more clearly on what is true and helpful. This means we also need the support of our meditation practice in working with the worldly winds. We need what is traditionally known as *śamatha* – a spiritual robustness, a reservoir of awareness and emotional positivity, resources that we can draw on when we're in the thick of it. Meditation practice and time on retreat are part of the supportive conditions that help build up that reservoir.

I used the teaching of the stages of Enlightenment to show how meditation can free up the energy we've invested in controlling or avoiding the worldly winds, and this energy can then be developed into equanimity.

6) Watching the winds of change

The worldly winds are the winds of change. Seeing them in this way, looking even more deeply into them, they can become 'wisdom teachers' or 'reality teachers'. They show us how life is constant change; when we resist or deny that change we create tension and frustration. But it is also possible to learn to soar with the winds of change and experience freedom.

7) Understanding the western worldly winds

Lastly, we examined scientism and consumerism – two of the stories or myths of our time that promise, through technology and material wealth, to create a heaven-haven in which the worldly winds can be controlled. Buddhist practice is about creating a better world, based on a more enlightened and aware attitude to the worldly winds.

I had four suggestions for practice in this area:

a) Self-development
b) Withdrawing support from institutions, groups and forces in society that perpetuate a limited, materialistic vision
c) Speaking out: critiquing limited ideologies, and communicating real vision and values
d) Joining a spiritual community and helping it to grow

The Buddhist path is often described as a threefold path of ethics, meditation and wisdom. Stages one to three described above, and to some extent stage four, represent ethics. Stage four and five represent meditation. Stage five is about the development of wisdom as well as meditation, and stage six is about wisdom. Stage seven takes us back to ethics again, looking at the way our culture implicitly promotes materialistic values and subtly undermines spiritual ones. It is looking at ethics as they manifest socially, culturally and collectively. It is more explicitly about 'transforming world', whereas the earlier material was more explicitly about 'transforming self', though of course it isn't really possible to separate the two. To transform world we need to transform ourselves, to cultivate more awareness, kindness, confidence, and so on. And to transform self we need to be aware of the world around us, how it affects and conditions us, and what role we are playing within it. The two are part of an overall process of transformation.

Reflection: Resolve – Remind – Review

Here's a last teaching for coursing the worldly winds, a really practical, nuts-and-bolts, toolbox for keeping your practice on course day-to-day, in the midst of a busy life. It is about creating the conditions that support practice; often we don't put sufficient supports in place and so our practice can run thin, or go off-beam. Rather prosaically, this teaching is called the three Rs: resolve, remind, review . . .

a) Resolve

First of all, make a clear resolve. What are you going to try to practise this week? You could go back to the reflections in chapters 1 to 3 to identify particular worldly winds that you especially want to watch out for, or specific 'Dharma-doors' that you want to try to find. Or you could choose to look out for, and work with, a different pair of worldly winds each week.

In other words, form some precepts – some principles and guidelines for training. Make them as specific as you can, not just general vague statements of your good intention. Be realistic – it's better to come up with one or two precepts that you'll actively engage with than ten big precepts that are likely to remain on the level of aspiration. Or rather, have the big aspiration, but remember it is also crucial to translate that into a few more practical propositions.

Record your resolutions somewhere, in a practice diary or notebook, so you can refer back to them.

b) Remind

Then we need reminders and supports for when we're in the midst of busyness that can distract us from our deeper purpose, for when the winds are blowing, or maybe when there's a storm. Here are three practical suggestions for reminders:

i) Slogans
Form your resolutions into really pithy (maybe even funny) slogans. Pin them up on your desk, or use those magnetic letters on your fridge to spell them out, or make them your computer screensaver for the week. You could also read books or poems, or listen to on-line Dharma talks, that are reminders of your true purpose.

ii) Rituals
Create rituals that also help to remind you. Perhaps have two-minute mindfulness breaks in your day. Or chant a mantra[61] whilst walking to work, or every time you are using the lift at the office. At home, you can have readings and reflections that relate to and deepen your resolutions. Or wear something that reminds you of them, or create a special shrine.

iii) Friends
Ask a like-minded friend to 'buddy-up' with you for a week or so, so you can talk to each other about your resolutions and progress in practising them. Make a date with them; don't just leave it that one of you will contact the other, as you know what will happen then! Meet for coffee, or chat on the telephone or, at the very least, text each other. Meeting and talking will also act as a reminder and a support.

c) Review

Lastly, review. Each day or two, ask yourself how it is going. Are my precepts proving helpful and realistic? Am I learning anything? Do I need to refine the precepts – perhaps making them a bit more specific, or adjusting the precept to take into account what I've learned so far? Do I need to be a bit more realistic, or could I be more ambitious? Shall I focus on fewer worldly winds, or just one precept?

You can make notes in your diary about how it is going – both your daily practice and also your meditation practice. You could do a quick daily review, and then a more in-depth weekly review. This will help you be more aware of what you've learned – both the successes and the need for more practice. It will also strengthen resolve for the future, taking you back to the first stage again.

Although early on in our spiritual life there are some things that seem to change quite quickly, most change is slow and subtle. There are highs and lows of practice, but there can also be long periods where you are trundling along and it all seems pretty ordinary. As long as you're engaged in what you're doing, that is probably OK, but if it goes on like that for too long you may want to introduce more of a stretch and challenge into your life and practice.

Change isn't always noticeable; sometimes we don't give ourselves credit for the changes we've made, because we simply don't notice them. We get used to ourselves, and think this is how we've always been. Sometimes it is our friends and acquaintances who reflect back to us how much we've changed.

We can also tend to perfectionism in practice, wanting to get it exactly right, and then swinging into defeatism when we don't, thinking we'll never change. Perfectionism, thinking that anything less than perfect is total failure, is a subtle form of eternalism (the belief in a perfect, unchanging state). Defeatism, thinking 'It was less than perfect, so I failed', is a subtle form of nihilism (the belief that things, in the end, come to nothing). Buddhism rejects both these views, because they are both equally static and fail to realize that life is a continuous process of making and re-making. In fact, you could see perfectionism and defeatism as another pair of worldly winds; creativity could be the Dharma-door that rises above them.

You can't avoid the worldly winds, but you can learn from them, and see them as opportunities rather than obstacles. As William Blake wrote:

> *Man was made for Joy & Woe;*
> *And when this we rightly know*
> *Thro' the world we safely go.*
> *Joy & Woe are woven fine,*
> *A Clothing for the soul Divine;*
> *Under every grief and pine*
> *Runs a joy with silken twine.*[62]

When we know that both pleasures and pains are part of the fabric of life, part of its warp and weft, we can weave something from them. Then they can be 'soul-making' (to use poetic rather than traditionally Buddhist language). They can teach us about the texture of life. They can reveal its heights and depths. They can show us to ourselves at our noblest and at our most petty. They can draw from us new qualities and dimensions of being.

To return to the metaphor of the wind, with awareness and skilfulness we can learn to sail the worldly winds, to ride the storms of life more safely. Though the worldly winds may howl and rage around us, we are more able to remain centred and calm. We retain perspective. We have a quiet confidence that whatever happens, we will know what to do, and things will be well. We keep hold of the 'silken twine' that weaves its way through the rush and roar of the worldly winds.

If . . .

This is of incalculable benefit to us, and it also helps others. Panic is contagious. If we get into a flap in a difficult situation, those around us are more likely to feel anxious and fearful. Other negative emotions like blaming or resentment likewise tend to poison the atmosphere, and other people have to breathe them in. But it works both ways. If we are more calm and confident, it will help others be so too. If we've got a perspective on what's going on, other people will pick up on that, at least to some extent.

I mentioned at the start of this book that I wrote it during the last few weeks of my father's life, working on it in the mornings, visiting him in hospital in the afternoons. Joy and woe were woven fine. They were difficult, sad weeks, and yet there was also something wonderful, precious, tender and human about them. Even now, some weeks later, when I close my eyes I immediately see my dad's face light up as we walk into the hospital ward. I hear some of the funny things he said. There are moments, little incidents, which I'll never forget.

Early one morning we got a call from the hospital – the one we knew was coming sooner or later. My dad had got much weaker in the night and they advised us to come in as quickly as we could. The car windscreen was covered in thick frost and ice which we hacked at with cold, fumbling fingers, until a friend came with a kettle of boiling water to melt the ice. We piled into the car and sped off. In the hospital we sat and held his hands as he took his last juddering breaths. He died very peacefully.

I'm still absorbing the impact of all this. It will be with me for the rest of my life. I'm so grateful for the teachings and practices of the Buddha that have given me a way to understand and work with what happened. Being with my father as he died has made death less strange, dark and unknown, and less frightening. It was as if he knew how to die, though he was a quiet, reserved man who did not talk about such things. I thought I was there to help him, but I was left feeling humbled and inspired by what he taught me about how to live and how to die.

As we travel through life we'll sometimes be able to soar with the worldly winds, and at other times they will be too strong and we will have to batten down the hatches and weather the storm. Either way involves knowing when to give up on our desires and attachments, going with the wind, rather than fighting against it.

Then, at the end of our travels, we will have to let go completely. We will have to give up all gain, praise, fame, pleasure – none of them will hold the same meaning for us any more. The more skilfully we've learned to sail the worldly winds in this life, the more we will be trained and prepared for that next journey. We'll know what to do. We'll find a way safely through.

The Buddha's teaching of the worldly winds

(The Lokavipatti Sutta translated from the Pali by Thanissaro Bhikkhu)[63]

'Monks, these eight worldly conditions spin after the world, and the world spins after these eight worldly conditions. Which eight? Gain, loss, status, disgrace, censure, praise, pleasure, & pain. These are the eight worldly conditions that spin after the world, and the world spins after these eight worldly conditions.

'For an uninstructed run-of-the-mill person there arise gain, loss, status, disgrace, censure, praise, pleasure, & pain. For a well-instructed disciple of the noble ones there also arise gain, loss, status, disgrace, censure, praise, pleasure, & pain. So what difference, what distinction, what distinguishing factor is there between the well-instructed disciple of the noble ones and the uninstructed run-of-the-mill person?'

'For us, lord, the teachings have the Blessed One as their root, their guide, & their arbitrator. It would be good if the Blessed One himself would explicate the meaning of this statement. Having heard it from the Blessed One, the monks will remember it.'

'In that case, monks, listen & pay close attention. I will speak.'

'As you say, lord,' the monks responded.

The Blessed One said, 'Gain arises for an uninstructed run-of-the-mill person. He does not reflect, 'Gain has arisen for me. It is inconstant, stressful, & subject to change.' He does not discern it as it actually is.

'Loss arises. . . Status arises. . . Disgrace arises. . . Censure arises. . . Praise arises. . . Pleasure arises. . .

'Pain arises. He does not reflect, 'Pain has arisen for me. It is inconstant, stressful, & subject to change.' He does not discern it as it actually is.

'His mind remains consumed with the gain. His mind remains consumed with the loss. . . with the status. . . the disgrace. . . the censure. . . the praise. . . the pleasure. His mind remains consumed with the pain.

'He welcomes the arisen gain and rebels against the arisen loss. He welcomes the arisen status and rebels against the arisen disgrace. He welcomes the arisen praise and rebels against the arisen censure. He welcomes the arisen pleasure and rebels against the arisen pain. As he is thus engaged in welcoming & rebelling, he is not released from birth, aging, or death; from sorrows, lamentations, pains, distresses, or despairs. He is not released, I tell you, from suffering & stress.

'Now, gain arises for a well-instructed disciple of the noble ones. He reflects, 'Gain has arisen for me. It is inconstant, stressful, & subject to change.' He discerns it as it actually is.

'Loss arises. . . Status arises. . . Disgrace arises. . . Censure arises. . . Praise arises. . . Pleasure arises. . .

'Pain arises. He reflects, 'Pain has arisen for me. It is inconstant, stressful, & subject to change.' He discerns it as it actually is.

'His mind does not remain consumed with the gain. His mind does not remain consumed with the loss. . . with the status. . . the disgrace. . . the censure. . . the praise. . . the pleasure. His mind does not remain consumed with the pain.

'He does not welcome the arisen gain, or rebel against the arisen loss. He does not welcome the arisen status, or rebel against the arisen disgrace. He does not welcome the arisen praise, or rebel against the arisen censure. He does not welcome the arisen pleasure, or rebel against the arisen pain. As he thus abandons welcoming & rebelling, he is released from birth, ageing, & death; from sorrows, lamentations, pains, distresses, & despairs. He is released, I tell you, from suffering & stress.

'This is the difference, this the distinction, this the distinguishing factor between the well-instructed disciple of the noble ones and the uninstructed run-of-the-mill person.'

Notes and References

1   The Buddha's main teaching on the worldly winds is found
     in the *Lokavipatti Sutta*, *Aṅguttara Nikāya*, 8.6, quoted in full on
     pp.109–11.

2   Sangharakshita, *Who is the Buddha?*, Windhorse Publications,
     1994, p.114.

3   M.D. Herter Norton (trans.), Rainer Maria Rilke, *Letters to a
     Young Poet*, W.W. Norton and Company, 1954, p.35.

4   This is a great book on how to reflect: Ratnaguna, *The Art of
     Reflection*, Windhorse Publications, 2010.

5   For more on 'blame' see, Nancy Baker, 'The Seventh Zen
     Precept: Not Elevating Oneself and Blaming Others', in *Tricycle*,
     Winter 2010.

6   RJ Hollingdale (ed.), *A Nietzsche Reader*, Penguin Books 1977,
     p.151.

7   *Mahāparinibbāna Sutta*, in Maurice Walshe (trans.), *Dīgha Nikāya*,
     Wisdom Publications, 1995, pp.231-290.

8   *op. cit.*, p.245.

9   *Ukkacela Sutta*, quoted in Vishvapani Blomfield, *Gautama
     Buddha: The Life and Teachings of the Awakened One*, Quercus,
     2011, p.272.

10 *Mahāparinibbāna Sutta* , *op. cit.*, p.265.

11 *op. cit.*, p.266.

12 See Karen Armstrong, *Buddha*, Phoenix, 2002, pp.148ff.

13 See for example, *Mahāsāropama Sutta, Majjhima Nikāya*, 29.

14 Sangharakshita *The Ten Pillars of Buddhism*, Windhorse Publications, 1989, pp.55-63.

15 Alain de Botton, *Status Anxiety*, Vintage, 2005, p.107.

16 *op. cit.*, p.108.

17 *Udāna* 4.8, in FL Woodward (trans.), *The Minor Anthologies of the Pali Canon*, Pali Text Society, 1985, pp.52–54.

18 *op. cit.*, p.52.

19 See *Udāna* 4.8/42-45.

20 Quoted in Bhikkhu Ñāṇamoli, *The Life of the Buddha*, Buddhist Publication Society, 1992, p.8.

21 There is a brief and simple description of this incident in the Pali texts (*Mahāsaccaka Sutta, Majjhima Nikāya*, 36). In later Buddhist tradition the story was elaborated on – see for example Aśvaghoṣa's *Buddhacarita, 5*.

22 *Sakkapañha Sutta*, in Walshe, *op.cit*, p.329.

23 *Salla Sutta, Saṃyutta Nikāya*, 36.6.

24 Vidyamala Burch, *Living Well with Pain and Illness: The Mindful Way to Free Yourself from Suffering*, Piatkus, 2008, pp.42–43.

25 www.breathworks-mindfulness.co.uk

26 *Parinibbāna Sutta*, *op. cit.*, p.257.

27 *Lokavipatti Sutta, Aṅguttara Nikāya*, 8.6.

28 See, for example, *The Honeyball Sutta*, Bhikkhu Ñāṇamoli and Bhikhi Bodhi (trans.), *Majjhima Nikāya*, 18, Wisdom Publications, 2005, pp. 201–206.

29 These are the seven *bodhyaṅgas*. *Bodhi* literally means 'awake', but is also often translated as 'Enlightened'. *Aṅga* is a 'limb' or 'shoot'. So I have rendered the *bodhyaṅgas* as the 'stages of Enlightenment'. For a reference to them in the traditional texts, see, for example, *The Ānāpānasati Sutta, Majjhima Nikāya*, 118, which has a section on the *bojjhaṅgas* as they are in the Pali. Since the Sanskrit *bodhyaṅgas* is more familiar, we'll be using Sanskrit terms in this chapter.

30 Excerpt from William Blake, 'The Marriage of Heaven and Hell', in *Blake Complete Writings*, edited by Geoffrey Keynes, Oxford University Press, 1972, p.149.

31 Sangharakshita, *Mind Reactive and Creative*, Windhorse Publications, 1995, p.20.

32 Sangharakshita, *What is the Dharma?*, Windhorse Publications, 1998, p.135.

33 *Dhammapada* 34.

34 Ayya Khema, *Who is Myself?*, Wisdom Publications, 1997, p.69.

35 Samuel Beckett, *Waiting for Godot*, Faber and Faber, 1971, p.69.

36 See, for example, *The Mahāhatthipadopama Sutta,* in *Majjhima Nikāya*, Bhikkhu Ñāṇamoli and Bhikhi Bodhi, *op. cit.*, pp.278–285, and also note 332.

37 The five precepts are the most well-known ethical guidelines in the Buddhist tradition: not to kill, not to take the not-given, to avoid sexual misconduct, not to speak that which is untrue, and to avoid that which intoxicates the mind.

38 I'm using the word 'ideological' in its Marxist sense – an idea that claims to be neutral, but actually contains assumptions and biases.

39 Bryan Appleyard, *Understanding the Present: Science and the Soul of Modern Man*, Pan Macmillan, 1992, p.2.

40 David Loy, *A Buddhist History of the West, op. cit.*, p.197.

41 David Loy, *Money, Sex, War, Karma, op. cit.*, p.126.

42 Bryan Magee, *Confessions of a Philosopher: A Journey Through Western Philosophy*, Phoenix, 1998, p.218.

43 Quoted in Bryan Appleyard, *op.cit.*, p.16.

44 Bryan Magee, *op. cit.*, p.200.

45 David Loy, *A Buddhist History of the West, op. cit.*, p.209.

46 Richard Layard, *Happiness: Lessons from a New Science*, Penguin, 2005, p.42.

47 *op. cit.*, p.50.

48 *op. cit.*, p. 48.

49 *op. cit.*, p.45.

50 Alain de Botton, *op. cit.*, p.194.

51 Pema Chödrön, *The Places that Scare You*, Shambhala, 2002, p.137.

52 David Brazier, *The New Buddhism: a Rough Guide to a New Way of Life*, Robinson, 2001, p.222.

53 Leo Braudy, *The Frenzy of Renown: Fame and its History*, Vintage, 1997, p8

54 David Loy, *Money, Sex, War, Karma*, *op. cit.*, p.35.

55 Leo Braudy, *op. cit.*, p.592.

56 I've adapted these from Sangharakshita, 'A Buddhist View of Current World Problems', in *What is the Sangha? The Nature of Spiritual Community*, Windhorse Publications, 2000, p.239ff.

57 Sangharakshita, *op. cit.*, p240.

58 The first of the Buddhist five precepts is not to kill or harm other life.

59 http://www.vegsoc.org/page.aspx?pid=520

60 Excerpt from Rudyard Kipling, 'If – ', quoted in Nicholas Albery (ed.), *Poem for the Day*, Sinclair-Stevenson, 1997, p.381.

61 *op. cit.*, p.50.

62 Excerpt from William Blake, 'Auguries of Innocence', in *Blake Complete Writings*, *op. cit.*, p.432.

63 Thanissaro Bhikkhu (trans.), *Lokavipatti Sutta, Aṅguttara Nikāya*, 8.6, at www.accesstoinsight.org

Windhorse Publications is a Buddhist publishing house, staffed by practising Buddhists. We place great emphasis on producing books of high quality which are accessible and relevant to those interested in Buddhism at whatever level. Drawing on the whole range of the Buddhist tradition, our books include translations of traditional texts, commentaries, books that make links with Western culture and ways of life, biographies of Buddhists, and works on meditation.

As a charitable institution we welcome donations to help us continue our work. We also welcome manuscripts on aspects of Buddhism or meditation. To join our mailing list, place an order, or request a catalogue please visit our website at www. windhorsepublications.com or contact:

Windhorse Publications Ltd.   Perseus Distribution
169 Mill Road   1094 Flex Drive
Cambridge CB1 3AN   Jackson TN 38301
UK   USA
info@windhorsepublications.com

Windhorse Books
PO Box 574
Newtown NSW 2042
Australia

Windhorse Publications is an arm of the Triratna Buddhist Community, which has more than sixty centres on five continents. Through these centres, members of the Triratna Buddhist Community offer regular programmes of events for the general public and for more experienced students. These include meditation classes, public talks, study on Buddhist themes and texts, and bodywork classes such as t'ai chi, yoga, and massage. Triratna also run several retreat centres and the Karuna Trust, a fundraising charity that supports social welfare projects in the slums and villages of Southern Asia.

Many Triratna centres have residential spiritual communities and ethical businesses associated with them. Arts activities are encouraged too, as is the development of strong bonds of friendship between people who share the same ideals. In this way Triratna is developing a unique approach to Buddhism, not simply as a set of techniques, but as a creatively directed way of life for people living in the modern world.

If you would like more information about Triratna please visit www.thebuddhistcentre.org or write to:

London Buddhist Centre
51 Roman Road
London E2 0HU
UK

Aryaloka
14 Heartwood Circle
Newmarket NH 03857
USA

Sydney Buddhist Centre
24 Enmore Road
Sydney NSW 2042
Australia

Also by Vajragupta

Buddhism: Tools for Living Your Life

In this guide for all those seeking a meaningful spiritual path, Vajragupta provides clear explanations of the main Buddhist teachings, as well as a variety of exercises designed to help readers develop or deepen their practice.

Appealing, readable, and practical, blending accessible teachings, practices, and personal stories . . . as directly relevant to modern life as it is comprehensive and rigorous. – Tricycle: The Buddhist Review, 2007

I'm very pleased that someone has finally written this book! At last, a real 'toolkit' for living a Buddhist life, his practical suggestions are hard to resist! – Saddhanandi, Chair of Taraloka Retreat Centre

Windhorse Publications
ISBN 9781 899579 74 7
£10.99 / $16.95 / €16.95
192 pages

The Triratna Story: Behind the Scenes of a New Buddhist Movement

This is the story of a circle of friends dreaming a dream, and working to make it a reality. It's the nitty-gritty tale of how a community evolves. It's a record of idealism and naivety, growth and growing pains, hard work and burn-out, friendship and fall-out. It's a celebration of how so much was achieved in so short a time, and a reflection on the mistakes made, and lessons learnt.

An excellent synopsis of the history of an important Buddhist movement. – David Brazier, author and head of the Amida-Shu.

. . .a courageous and important book. – Zoketsu Norman Fischer, author and founder of the Everyday Zen Foundation.

ISBN 9781 899579 92 1
£7.99 / $13.95 / €8.95
224 pagess

Also from Windhorse Publications

A Guide to the Buddhist Path
by Sangharakshita

The Buddhist tradition, with its numerous schools and teachings, can understandably feel daunting. Which teachings really matter? How can one begin to practice Buddhism in a systematic way? This can be confusing territory. Without a guide one can easily get dispirited or lost.

Profoundly experienced in Buddhist practice, intimately familiar with its main schools, and founder of the Triratna Buddhist Community, Sangharakshita is the ideal guide. In this highly readable anthology he sorts out fact from myth and theory from practice to reveal the principle ideals and teachings of Buddhism. The result is a reliable and far-reaching guide to this inspiring path.

ISBN 9781 907314 05 6
£16.99 / $23.95 / €19.95
264 pages

The Buddha's Noble Eightfold Path
by Sangharakshita

The Noble Eightfold Path is the most widely known of the Buddha's teachings. It is ancient, extending back to the Buddha's first discourse and is highly valued as a unique treasury of wisdom and practical guidance on how to live our lives.

This introduction takes the reader deeper while always remaining practical, inspiring and accessible. Sangharakshita translates ancient teachings and makes them relevant to the way we live our lives today.

Probably the best 'life coaching' manual you'll ever read, the key to living with clarity and awareness. – Karen Robinson, *The Sunday Times*

ISBN 9781 899579 81 5
£9.99 / $16.95 / €16.95
176 pages

Visions of Mahayana Buddhism
by Nagapriya

In a unique overview of this inspiring tradition, Nagapriya introduces its themes and huge spectrum of practices, literature, and movements. Charting the evolution and expression of the Mahayana as a whole, he tracks its movement across South and East Asia, uncovering its history, culture, and doctrines and blending this extensive knowledge with a strong element of lived practice.

Ideal for both teaching and personal use, this far-reaching and imaginative guide provides a solid foundation for any study in Buddhism and a valuable voice on Asian history.

A very helpful introduction and overview of this complex, fascinating tradition. – David R. Loy, author of *Money, Sex, War, Karma*

ISBN 9781 899579 97 6
£12.99 / $21.95 / €16.95
288 pages

A Path for Parents
by Sara Burns

A Path for Parents is for anyone interested in spiritual life within the context of parenting. Sara Burns, mother and Buddhist practitioner, draws on her own experience to deliver a refreshingly honest and accessible account of how parents can grow spiritually among their everyday experiences of life with children.

ISBN 9781 899579 70 9
£11.99 / $17.95 / €17.95
176 pages

The Three Jewels series
by Sangharakshita

This set of three essential texts introduces the Three Jewels which are central to Buddhism: the *Buddha* (the Enlightened One), the *Dharma* (the Buddha's teachings), and the *Sangha* (the spiritual community).

Who is the Buddha?

ISBN 9781 899579 51 8
£8.99 / $14.95 / €11.95
188 pages

What is the Dharma?

ISBN 9781 899579 01 3
£9.99 / $19.95 / €12.95
272 pages

What is the Sangha?

ISBN 9781 899579 31 0
£9.99 / $19.95 / €12.95
288 pages

Meeting the Buddhas series

by Vessantara

This set of three informative guides, by one of our best-selling authors, introduces the historical and archetypal figures from within the Tibetan Buddhist tradition. Each book focuses on a different set of figures and features full-colour illustrations.

A Guide to the Buddhas

ISBN 9781 899579 83 9
£11.99 / $18.95 / €18.95
176 pages

A Guide to the Bodhisattvas

ISBN 9781 899579 84 6
£11.99 / $18.95 / €18.95
128 pages

A Guide to the Deities of the Tantra

ISBN 9781 899579 85 3
£11.99 / $18.95 / €18.95
192 pages

Buddhist Wisdom in Practice **series**

The Art of Reflection
by Ratnaguna

It is all too easy either to think obsessively, or to not think enough.
But how do we think usefully? How do we reflect? Like any
art, reflection can be learnt and developed, leading to a deeper
understanding of life and to the fullness of wisdom. *The Art of
Reflection* is a practical guide to reflection as a spiritual practice,
about "what we think and how we think about it". It is a book
about contemplation and insight, and reflection as a way to
discover the truth.

*No-one who takes seriously the study and practice of the Dharma should
fail to read this ground-breaking book.* – Sangharakshita, founder of the
Triratna Buddhist Community

ISBN 9781 899579 89 1
£9.99 / $16.95 / €11.95
160 pages

This Being, That Becomes
by Dhivan Thomas Jones

Dhivan Thomas Jones takes us into the heart of the Buddha's
insight that everything arises in dependence on conditions. With
the aid of lucid reflections and exercises he prompts us to explore
how conditionality works in our own lives, and provides a sure
guide to the most essential teaching of Buddhism.

Clearly and intelligently written, this book carries a lot of good advice.
Prof Richard Gombrich, author of *What the Buddha Thought*.

ISBN 9781 899579 90 7
£12.99 / $20.95 / €15.95
216 pages